CONSTELLATIONS

Like the future itself, the imaginative possibilities of science fiction are limitless. And the very development of cinema is inextricably linked to the genre, which, from the earliest depictions of space travel and the robots of silent cinema to the immersive 3D wonders of contemporary blockbusters, has continually pushed at the boundaries. **Constellations** provides a unique opportunity for writers to share their passion for science fiction cinema in a book-length format, each title devoted to a significant film from the genre. Writers place their chosen film in a variety of contexts – generic, institutional, social, historical – enabling **Constellations** to map the terrain of science fiction cinema from the past to the present... and the future.

'This stunning, sharp series of books fills a real need for authoritative, compact studies of key science fiction films. Written in a direct and accessible style by some of the top critics in the field, brilliantly designed, lavishly illustrated and set in a very modern typeface that really shows off the text to best advantage, the volumes in the **Constellations** series promise to set the standard for SF film studies in the 21st century.'
Wheeler Winston Dixon, Ryan Professor of Film Studies, University of Nebraska

 Constellations

 Constelbooks

Also available in this series

12 Monkeys Susanne Kord

Blade Runner Sean Redmond

Brainstorm Joseph Maddrey

Children of Men Dan Dinello

Close Encounters of the Third Kind Jon Towlson

The Damned Nick Riddle

Dune Christian McCrea

Ex Machina Joshua Grimm

Inception David Carter

Jurassic Park Paul Bullock

Lost Brigid Cherry

The OA David Sweeney

Mad Max Martyn Conterio

Minority Report D. Harlan Wilson

Mr. Freedom Tyler Sage

RoboCop Omar Ahmed

Rollerball Andrew Nette

Seconds Jez Conolly & Emma Westwood

Stalker Jon Hoel

The Stepford Wives Samantha Lindop

CONSTELLATIONS

Moon

Brian J. Robb

First published in 2023 by
Auteur, an imprint of
Liverpool University Press,
4 Cambridge Street,
Liverpool L69 7ZU
www.liverpooluniversitypress.co.uk/imprints/Auteur/
Copyright © Auteur 2023

Series design: Nikki Hamlett at Cassels Design
Set by Cassels Design, Luton, UK.

All rights reserved. No part of this publication may be reproduced in any material form (including photocopying or storing in any medium by electronic means and whether or not transiently or incidentally to some other use of this publication) without the permission of the copyright owner.

British Library Cataloguing-in-Publication Data
A catalogue record for this book is available from the British Library

ISBN hardback: 9781800856424
ISBN Paperback: 9781800856431
eISBN: 9781800855199

Contents

Chapter 1: From Space Oddity to Space Odyssey 7

Chapter 2: Isolation and Identity 27

Chapter 3: The Look of the Future 51

Chapter 4: The Theology of *Moon* 71

Chapter 5: 'We are not programmed!' 91

Bibliography & Works Cited 113

Chapter I: From Space Oddity to Space Odyssey

'Everything I am is a reflection of the experiences I went through growing up, whether the films, or the music my dad played .... I came from a very unique time and place. That made me who I am.'[1] – Duncan Jones.

Moon (2009), co-written and directed by Duncan Jones, tells a relatively simple story on the surface, but the text of the film can be mined – just as the central character, Sam Bell (Sam Rockwell), mines Helium-3 on the dark side of the moon – for depth and hidden meaning. The film is an example of creativity born out of constraints, a process typical of the low-budget British film industry. It presents situations and characters that throw up ethical questions that can be examined for philosophical depths. None of this would be reaching for dubious meaning, either. The screenplay, by Nathan Parker based upon an original story from Jones, is deft in setting up situations and character, but it leaves enough space for the viewer to apply their own meaning to what is seen on screen. In this way, and many others (as will be explored), *Moon* is a throwback to such 1970s and 1980s serious and philosophical science-fiction films as *Silent Running* (1972), *Soylent Green* (1973), *Logan's Run* (1976), *Alien* (1979), and *Outland* (1981), all of which were influences on Jones. The film is also the result of a collaborative process between Jones, Rockwell, and such key figures as conceptual designer Gavin Rothery (who went on to write and direct 2020's *Archive*, a clear descendant of *Moon*), and special effects legend Bill Pearson (*Flash Gordon*, 1980). Just as the moon so often visible above Earth has been interpreted in a variety of ways throughout human history, so the film *Moon* is open to various readings and interpretations.

This opening chapter will cover the early filmmaking and influences of *Moon* director Duncan Jones, examining his position – creatively and personally – as the son of music pioneer David Bowie, and briefly look at past depictions of the moon in science-fiction cinema. A production history of *Moon* lays the foundation for the in-depth study of later chapters, with a particular focus on how the constraints of British low-budget filmmaking inspire creativity. Chapter two examines questions of isolation and identity as raised in *Moon*: what defines a human being; how does differing experience change each of the Sam Bell clones; how important is family, community and human contact in a sense of the self; is a clone a 'person' in terms of 'human rights'; what is the future of the individual in the world of work; what role do corporations and planetary need play; and is cloning a viable solution to work in hostile environments? Additionally, the role of Gerty, Sam's robotic assistant, will be examined in relation to the malevolent HAL 9000 in *2001: A Space Odyssey* (1968). Chapter three will focus on issues of design, especially how Duncan Jones and his creative team envisioned the future in *Moon*, from the look of the sets, and the diverse equipment and vehicles featured, through to costume design and even typography, and how it was all used in service of the overall themes. Chapter four will tackle issues of theology through *Moon* by examining notions of curiosity and investigation (asking the right questions); religion and reason; work and reward; dehumanisation and corporate greed; ignorance versus knowledge; deception and self-deception; information control and the manufacture of belief; empathy and the capacity for *caritas*; and the role of the 'scapegoat' as reflected in *Moon*. Finally, in chapter five the critical reception of *Moon* will be examined, while the way the film's themes were further developed and extrapolated upon in Duncan Jones' next film, *Source Code* (2011), will also be considered. The career trajectory of Jones in the aftermath of *Moon* will be studied, revealing that many of the concerns of his debut feature film continue to appear in his later, much bigger budgeted film work.

Filmmaker Duncan Jones began life in 1971 with the unlikely moniker of 'Zowie Bowie'. His birth also resulted in the creation of two songs: 'Kooks' and 'Oh! You Pretty Things'. Of course, both of these were the direct result of Jones being the son of singer-songwriter David Bowie. Formally named Duncan Zowie Haywood Jones, he went by the wacky name 'Zowie' until the cusp of his teenage years when self-consciousness no doubt kicked in. The younger Jones (his father's birth name being David Jones) was not particularly close with either of his parents when they were together, although he grew closer to his father in later years. He was the only son of David and Angie Bowie, American model and actress. Growing up across Europe – London, Berlin, Switzerland – Duncan was often an afterthought in his parents' lives, mainly being the responsibility of his Scottish nanny, Marion Skene.

His parents' divorce in 1980, when Duncan was aged eight, had a traumatic impact on him. His father gained custody, and around the same time Jones dropped 'Zowie'. Jones also cut off all contact with his mother. From the age of 14, while attending the Scottish boarding school Gordonstoun in Moray (from which he was ultimately expelled), Duncan was instead known as 'Joey' or 'Joe'. When he attended his father's wedding to second wife model Iman (Zara Mohamed Abdulmajid) in 1992, he was still 'Joe'. It wasn't until he turned 18 that he reverted to his given name of Duncan Jones, a decision that allowed him some distance from his celebrity parents.

All this might suggest questions of identity would come as second nature to Duncan Jones, and they are at the heart of *Moon*. His mother, Angie Bowie, could certainly see something of the real life of her troubled son in his debut movie. 'What upset me is how powerful and personal it is,' she said to the *Mail on Sunday*.[2] 'It is all about alienation and abandonment, and for the first time I realised how much grief I caused my son by letting him go. I now realise, through Zowie's art, what a mistake I made in leaving him.' Notably, Angie Bowie still refers to the adult Duncan as 'Zowie'.

Alienation, abandonment, isolation, and confusion are at the heart of *Moon*. The themes run through the movie from the first appearance of Sam Rockwell as Sam Bell, apparently alone on the moon, monitoring the mining of Helium-3 to provide energy for Earth. Questions of identity permeate the movie: how experience defines a person; the importance of family, community, and human contact to the sense of self; and the very definition of 'What is human?' Jones is a fan of American science-fiction author Philip K. Dick (his *Do Androids Dream of Electric Sheep*, 1968, was the source for Ridley Scott's *Blade Runner*, 1982), who often explored this question.

His formal film education came from the London International Film School, which Jones attended following a Bachelor's Degree in Philosophy from the College of Wooster in rural Ohio and an ultimately abandoned Ph.D. at Vanderbilt University in Tennessee. Both these previous pursuits of further education seem, in retrospect, to be a denial of what Jones was centrally interested in. Where David Bowie hoped his son would be a rock star like him, or – at the very least – a musician of some sort, Jones was always set upon being a filmmaker. He virtually grew up on film sets, joining his father during the shooting of Nicholas Roeg's *The Man Who Fell to Earth* in 1976 at the age of five, and enjoying the ingenuity behind the Jim Henson Creature

Shop creations on *Labyrinth* (1986) at a more mature 15. He later spent six months working for the Henson Creature Shop outpost in London's trendy Camden Town.

Despite deliberately choosing to use a form of identity that disguised his relationship to Bowie, Jones was not above using that connection in his filmmaking apprenticeship. In 1997 he worked as a camera operator for music video director Tim Pope who was capturing footage of Bowie's 50th birthday celebrations held at Madison Square Gardens. He went on two years later to perform similar duties capturing footage of two of his father's concerts at the Roseland Ballroom in New York City in 2000. When his father was hosting the second season of Tony Scott's *The Hunger* television series (1997–2000, based on Scott's 1983 vampire movie that co-starred Bowie and Catherine Deneuve) in Montreal, Jones spent time on set filming pick-up footage for the production. Finally, Duncan Jones graduated from the London International Film School in 2001, aged 30.

One of Jones' earliest commercial creative works was the short *Blade Jogger*, a low budget homage to Scott's *Blade Runner*, starring *A Shot in the Dark's* (1964) Burt Kwouk, which won a top award in Kodak UK's Student Commercial Competition. Promoting Kodak's single-use disposable camera, the 30-second spot simulated *Blade Runner*'s rain-drenched future vision of Los Angeles, transported to London's Chinatown. The influence of *Blade Runner* on Jones' filmmaking would be even more pronounced in his Netflix feature *Mute* (2018).

Using money inherited from his late grandmother, Jones set out to make a more ambitious low budget short, both as a 'proof of concept' for a more sophisticated feature he had in mind and as a way of gaining further experience. He drew upon the talents of several people he'd worked with while dabbling in music videos (set dressing, rather than directing), video game 'cinematics' creation (for strategy game *Republic: The Revolution*, 2003), and in shooting test commercials. Several of these collaborators would work in key capacities on *Moon*, including effects editor Barrett Heathcote, art director Hideki Arichi, and concept artist Gavin Rothery. These four combined their talents to create *Whistle* (2002), a 30-minute movie shot on 35mm film.

Shot in Switzerland, *Whistle* focuses on the contrast between the everyday family life of Ryan (Dominic Mafham, *Humans* 2015–18) with his wife Diana (Sarah Winman, *Holby City* 1999–present) and young video-game playing son Michael (Charlie Hicks), and his work-from-home life as a 'digital assassin'. His handler, who dishes out his assignments, is played by veteran actor John Shrapnel (*Between the Lines*, 1992–94; he died in 2020, aged 77). When Ryan becomes troubled by the mistaken death of a child related to his target, he finds he's not as detached from the consequences of his 'work' as he'd previously believed. Science fictional, in that it employs a long-distance digitally driven method of assassination (a balcony-mounted missile launch system) that didn't quite exist in 2002, *Whistle* is perhaps more a precursor of Jones' work on *Moon* in the relationship between Ryan and Diana than in any other aspect. She is fully aware of his occupation (dispensing with one possible source of tension) and, in fact, picks up the pieces with Ryan's employer when he has qualms about his role. The film ends on an ambivalent note as Ryan attempts to make contact with the wife of his 'victims', seemingly leading to him becoming a target himself. Jones' dedication in the end credits – 'to Dads … everywhere' – was made long before he became a father in 2016, so can only be further testament to the bond between Jones and his own father. The credits run to the closing moments of the 1977 Bowie track 'Subterraneans'.

Following *Whistle* – which had sown the seeds of Jones' feature filmmaking ambitions – the director spent some time working in advertising. Since the late-1970s and early 1980s, advertising had become a proven route into filmmaking for a range of British creative talents, including Alan Parker (father of *Moon* screenwriter Nathan Parker), Ridley Scott, Tony Scott, and Hugh Hudson – several of these talents would be involved in Jones' career and, especially, in the genesis of *Moon*. Jones began working for ad man Trevor Beattie at the agency Beattie McGuinness Bungay (BMB), making his commercials debut in 2005 with a controversial French Connection advert. This was also the first film co-produced by Jones' Liberty Films shingle, a company he'd set up with Stuart Fenegan, an up-and-coming producer he'd met shortly after making *Whistle*. The French Connection ad, styled as 'Fashion vs. Style' depicted two women, representing those notions, fighting then kissing (it was inevitably dubbed the 'kung-fu lesbian advert'). When the ad debuted in February 2006, it attracted almost 130 complaints to the Advertising Standards Authority.

For the next two-and-a-half years, Beattie gave Jones a filmmaking home, a place to practise his craft and extend his abilities. He made ads for Heinz ketchup (one, entitled 'Seed', featured a CGI tomato plant that sprouted a ketchup bottle, that allowed him to explore the possibilities of visual effects), for Carling C2 ('Robots') that gave him the opportunity to debut a prototype version of Gerty, the robotic assistant from *Moon*, and for McCain oven chips ('A Year to Remember'), Game Cube ('Dreams'), Olympus ('Like A Memory', featuring Gerty voice actor Kevin Spacey), and Virgin Money ('40 Years of Better', covering the Virgin company's growth from *Tubular Bells* to Virgin Galactic). Jones noted his period in commercial advertising was 'long enough for me to learn, try out and experiment on a technical level. There was a lot for me to learn … when we did decide we were just going to go for it and make a feature film, Trevor [Beattie] was one of the first people I went to.'[3] Beattie would function as an executive producer on Jones' feature film debut.

The moon has long fascinated mankind and remains an important part of folklore, even after exhaustive scientific research and discovery. It is approximately 1/6th the size of Earth, and while its exact origins are still open to speculation (a rogue planetoid captured by Earth's gravity? A chunk of the Earth itself, blown off planet?), the moon is estimated to be around 4.6 billion years old. Visible almost every night (weather allowing), the moon remains a great unknown, a lure for mankind, and a sign of how little we've actually advanced into space as a species.

Stories about trips to the moon have been around as long as humanity has looked up into the night sky and wondered about Earth's nearest natural satellite. It's been over 50 since mankind finally stepped onto the surface after Neil Armstrong and Buzz Aldrin guided their *Eagle* lunar lander to a safe touchdown in the Sea of Tranquility in July 1969. In the decades before and after the Apollo missions, which spanned 1960 to 1972, filmmakers tried to capture what it might be like to travel to the moon. Prior to Apollo 11's landing on 20 July 1969, imagination was key – after all, no-one knew what the surface of the moon was really like. Afterwards, verisimilitude became paramount as filmmakers attempted to replicate the sights and sounds sent back by Armstrong and Aldrin.

Long before the Apollo missions of the 1960s and early 1970s, movies took humanity to the moon. French film pioneer Georges Méliès drew upon the work of early science-fiction authors Jules Verne (*From the Earth to the Moon*, 1865; *Around the Moon*, 1870) and H. G. Wells (*The First Men in the Moon*, 1901) with 1902's *La Voyage dans la Lune* (*A Trip to the Moon*). Inventive in technique and wildly influential, Méliès' short was just one of an estimated 500 or so he made between 1896 and 1913, many of them now lost.

Méliès dabbled in every genre, from basic trick films (*The Man With the Rubber Head*, 1901), to exploration (*The Conquest of the Pole*, 1912) and horror (*The Devil's Castle*, 1896). It is no surprise, then, that he should also pioneer the science-fiction movie. Méliès used every technique at his disposal, including substitution cuts, multiple exposure, time-lapse photography, cross dissolves, and hand-coloured prints to achieve the seemingly impossible. In the film's most famous – and often copied – image, the space capsule slams into the eye of the 'man in the moon'. Méliès secured his place in film history with this and several other films, but it is that image of the face of the moon with the capsule embedded in its eye that most people know.

Taking his cue from Méliès, Fritz Lang avoided fantasy and adopted the 1920s version of 'realism' for *Frau im Mond* (1929, *Woman on the Moon*). Drawn from a novel by Lang's partner, Thea von Harbou titled *The Rocket to the Moon*, this was Lang's follow up to *Metropolis* (1927). Lang painstakingly depicted the process of launching a rocket, anticipating the Apollo programme. The rocket is built upright, then moved to the launch pad, where a countdown featured prior to lift-off – the first movie to do this. Perhaps the most startlingly accurate prediction from Lang was the multi-stage rocket, with pristine model work depicting the rocket ejecting its initial stage and firing a second stage – this in the 1920s, long before any experimental launches in the real world. The film also depicts a fairly accurate experience of zero gravity. Although Lang moved far ahead of Méliès, his representation of the moon's surface featured huge mountain-scapes. Equal parts melodrama and sci-fi spectacle, *Frau im Mond* is best remembered for its realistic rockets than its love triangle, espionage shenanigans, and preposterous moon environment.

The depiction of a flight to the moon took a slight step back with 1936's H. G. Wells adaptation, *Things to Come*, in which a manned capsule is fired at the moon from a giant 'space gun'. The 'space gun' device, attacked by a group of anti-technologists, is a throwback to the propulsion ideas of Verne and Méliès, failing to build upon the realistic space launch system depicted by Lang.

Attempts to creatively depict such technological ingenuity in cinema were given a boost in the 1950s and 1960s, largely thanks to improved special effects and a better scientific understanding of what the moon might be like and what might be necessary to get there. Almost a decade before the first spacecraft surveyed the moon (the unmanned Soviet craft *Luna 2* touched down in 1959), producer George Pal got there first in *Destination Moon* (1950, loosely drawn from Robert Heinlein's novel *Rocket Ship Galileo*, 1947). Ahead of its time in depicting a privately financed trip – now all the rage with the likes of Jeff Bezos' Blue Origin, Richard Branson's Virgin Galactic, and Elon Musk's SpaceX – Irving Pichel's film painstakingly detailed the technology and dangers of space travel. When the *Destination Moon* crew land, they find themselves in a Chesley Bonestell landscape – his matte paintings feature throughout. His mountain-dominated lunar landscapes are impressive, even if the Apollo landings later proved them to be utterly unrealistic.

Almost as if in reaction to George Pal's painstakingly detailed moon voyage, *From the Earth to the Moon* (1958) reverted to Jules Verne fantasy. Star-studded, with Joseph Cotten, George Sanders, and Debra Paget, the film sees an American Civil War munitions manufacturer use Powder X, a new high explosive, to launch a ship to the moon. Released by Warner Bros. just a year after the launch of the Soviet satellite Sputnik, *From the Earth to the Moon* was one of the first Hollywood films able to capitalise on growing interest in space travel and questions about a trip to the moon.

The British production *First Men in the Moon* (1964) played the patriotism card by drawing upon H. G. Wells for this fun fantasy adventure. Eccentric Victorian scientist Joseph Cavor (Lionel Jeffries) invents an anti-gravity material he modestly calls 'Cavorite'. He builds a spherical ship that, once painted with Cavorite, he intends to launch to the moon. He is joined by playwright Arnold Bedford (Edward Judd) and, accidentally, Bedford's fiancé, Kate Callender (Martha Hyer). On the moon, the explorers discover an underground civilisation of insectoid-like creatures Cavor dubs

'Selenites' and their giant caterpillar-like 'Moon Calf'. Escaping to the surface, the pair find that their sphere (a Steampunk-style craft, in which they'd left Kate) has been taken by the Selenites. Cavor encounters the Grand Lunar, the Selenites' leader, and begins an intellectual debate with him until Bedford intervenes, attempting to blast the creature with his 'elephant gun'. Bedford and Kate flee in the ship, but Cavor remains behind. Ultimately, as revealed in a then-contemporary 1960s wraparound, Cavor's common cold virus killed off the Selenites (a similar viral infection saved humanity from invading Martians in Wells' 1898 novel *The War of the Worlds*).

When in 1964 Stanley Kubrick and Arthur C. Clarke embarked upon *2001: A Space Odyssey* very little was known about our solar system, beyond the moon. The moon landings were still some way off, and Mars and anything beyond were pretty much *terra incognito*. There was little actual science for the creators of *2001* to draw upon to envision what Kubrick described as the 'proverbial "good" science fiction movie'. Kubrick's painstaking masterpiece would be the artistic culmination of depictions of the moon in movies in the two decades prior to the actual moon landing.

Teaming with Clarke, Kubrick focused on the details of near-Earth space travel (making it almost mundane) while also expanding to take a cosmic perspective on mankind's first steps into space. Kubrick prepared by watching many space- and moon-themed films, learning vital lessons. He persuaded MGM to back his plan to make the most realistic space adventure ever conceived to the tune of $9 million, then an astronomical budget for a movie, and – just as importantly – he brought in NASA-experienced designers and engineers to create the various spacecraft.

The elements that make *2001* a lasting achievement are those that move past the realism of Kubrick's depiction of a trip to the moon (and beyond), including enigmatic and unknowable aliens, the rogue AI, HAL-9000, and – most complex of all – the climatic 'stargate' sequence and the 'birth' of the 'star child'. Critics and theorists, science-fiction writers and fans continue to debate the 'meaning' of the film to this day. Kubrick's film hit cinemas just one year before the touchdown of the lunar lander *Eagle*, conveying Armstrong and Aldrin to their historic 'giant leap'. It set a new standard for realism in the cinematic depiction of space travel, something that subsequent films were both beholden to and would, ultimately, react against.

While *2001: A Space Odyssey* wasn't the last movie to feature the moon, it was the apotheosis of the form. For much of the two decades between the 1970s and the 1990s, the moon was out of vogue as a science-fiction destination. The successful real-life Apollo programme drained the cinematic sense of wonder from Earth's nearest satellite. That realism reasserted itself as the Apollo moon landings became relegated to history. Fanciful science-fiction portrayals of a journey to the moon were replaced by the ultra-realistic depiction of Ron Howard's *Apollo 13* (1995) and the reverential television mini-series *From the Earth to the Moon* (1998).

Since *Moon* in 2009, there have been a handful of other lunar-themed films, including *Apollo 18* (2011) and *Iron Sky* (2012) which fall into the alternate history category of science fiction, which also encapsulates television series *For All Mankind* (2019–). The found footage-driven *Apollo 18* is built around an imaginary 1973 mission that seemingly encountered aliens, while *Iron Sky* is a comic camp concoction that speculates that Nazis established a moon base at the end of the Second World War and are now preparing their space fleet to invade Earth. The most realistic moon movie since *Moon* has been the Neil Armstrong bio-pic *First Man* (2018), starring Ryan Gosling.

The best movies inspired by mankind's desire to reach out to the moon are those that take a realistic approach – sections of *Frau im Mond*, *Destination Moon*, and *2001: A Space Odyssey* pointed in the direction that the likes of *Apollo 13*, *From the Earth to the Moon*, and *First Man* were to take. However, the most entertaining outings are those that take a fantastical approach to what remains a fantastic achievement, so the likes of the ultimately silly *First Men in the Moon* and the profound *2001: A Space Odyssey* have equal claim to fulfilling audience's lunacy.

From his father's 1969 song 'Space Oddity' (released during the summer of the first manned moon landing) to his favourite film, *2001: A Space Odyssey*, the making of *Moon* appears fated for Duncan Jones. However, the film only developed after his first attempt to get his initial screenplay, *Mute* (which wouldn't be made for another decade), into production failed. Looking to cast a rising star to attract financing, Jones had a meeting with actor Sam Rockwell. American-born Rockwell had made his big screen debut in the 1989 slasher movie *Clowntown* and had appeared in a variety of television guest roles throughout the 1990s, interspersed with small movie roles. It wasn't until the turn of the century that Rockwell achieved name recognition with a significant appearance in *Star Trek* spoof *Galaxy Quest* (1999), and the lead role as game-show-host-turned-spy Chuck Barris in *Confessions of a Dangerous Mind* (2002). Jones and Rockwell hit it off, but Rockwell wasn't interested in the antagonist role on offer in *Mute* (he feared typecasting in villain roles) and preferred the lead hero, Leo. Jones didn't see Rockwell in that part, but the pair parted friends. So keen was Jones to work with Rockwell, he set about drafting a new script tailor-made for the actor.

Working with his partners in Liberty Films, producer Stuart Fenegan and VFX expert and designer Gavin Rothery, Jones determined their project would have to be low-budget if it were to stand a chance of entering production – all three were untried filmmakers, despite their extensive preparatory experience. Aware of science-fiction film history, Jones decided he needed to emulate several signature films of the 1970s that had featured a more-or-less isolated protagonist in a single location. *Silent Running*, Douglas Trumbull's 1972 thoughtful eco fable, was largely built around Bruce Dern's Freeman Lowell, custodian of the last remaining Earth forests, held in geodesic domes on the spaceship *Valley Forge*. The film also featured a trio of charming non-humanoid service robots, dubbed Huey, Dewey, and Louie (after Donald Duck's nephews). Trumbull – who'd worked on the special effects for Kubrick's *2001: A Space Odyssey* – shot much of the cavernous space freighter interiors on the decommissioned Korean War-era aircraft carrier *USS Valley Forge*, then docked at the Long Beach Naval Shipyard prior to being scrapped. Also on Jones' mind were small cast films like John Carpenter's debut *Dark Star* (1974), Ridley Scott's *Alien*, and the Sean Connery outer space remake of *High Noon* (1952), *Outland* (directed by Peter Hyams). By early 2007, Jones and his embryonic production team had resolved to shoot a film featuring a single actor in a single location. Aware that the 40th anniversary of the 1969 moon landing was on the horizon, the team set themselves the target of getting their moon-based film released by the end of 2009.

The setting was germane to its hoped-for wide appeal. According to Jones: 'We've already been to the moon and it feels really tangible. You can look up in the sky and see it every night. Everybody globally has a relationship with the moon, which also makes it – even though it's sci-fi and even though there are these strange ideas in it –

feel really close and relevant. That's why we decided to base it there.'[4]

The entire team was pragmatic about what could be achieved in the low-budget arena in British filmmaking. A single location (even if a rather expansive one) and a single actor (even if he plays more than one version of his character) were central to the script that Jones and screenwriter Nathan Parker (son of British director Alan Parker, who died in 2020 aged 76) set out to write. Jones had drafted the basic storyline as a treatment in 2007 (while still working on commercials) and already had Sam Rockwell in mind to star. Producer Stuart Fenegan had to put together an attractive package that could be pitched to prospective investors to fund the production of the movie.

Nathan Parker was new to the *Moon* team and was hired as Jones and Fenegan would be busy with their 'day jobs' and didn't want to slow development on what they hoped would be their feature film debut. Parker had already scripted the thriller movie *Blitz*, based on the novel by Ken Bruen, but that wouldn't enter production until 2011, after *Moon* – which would serve as his debut screenplay. Parker had a first draft screenplay ready within a month of being hired. There was some slight tension between Jones and Parker to begin with, as Jones regarded the project idea as 'his baby' (according to Parker) and was concerned about handing it over to another writer.

Parker had prepared by watching a variety of science-fiction movies suggested by Jones, including Jones' own favourite *2001: A Space Odyssey*, *Solaris* (1972, remade in 2002), *Alien*, and *Blade Runner*. Parker's take was that the film could essentially take place anywhere (in a remote factory on Earth, for example) given the one 'sci-fi' conceit of cloning. Following Jones' guidance, it was Parker's job to focus on character and story rather than wider genre tropes.

While Jones worked on production design with Gavin Rothery (in whatever time he could spare), Fenegan attempted to put together a financing package suitable for the film they hoped to achieve. Jones was also feeding script notes to Parker, especially focusing on the character arcs of the various Sam Bells throughout the narrative. According to Fenegan, all involved were propelled along by their own 'naivety' about working in the British film industry. 'We were just going balls to the wall, assuming it was all going to be fine,' noted Fenegan[5] of the ad-hoc development period of *Moon*.

Fenegan created a package made up of the script, images of the moon from a photography book entitled *Full Moon* (2002, by Michael Light), and whatever pre-production designs they had managed to put together. This was submitted to potential investors, many of them contacts from their time in the commercials sector, in the hope of raising enough finance to make the movie. Those who got involved early included Jones' advertising mentor Trevor Beattie and Trudie Styler, an actress-turned-producer who'd been helping develop new British filmmaking talent since the 1990s. The initial investors were happy for the film to move into production mode, beginning with set building, even though not all the finance nor a distribution deal had yet been finalised. This initiative actually helped secure the final phase of funding, as Jones and his team were able to approach potential distributors with photography and video of set building underway at Shepperton Studios. This made *Moon* appear more of a sure thing, and helped give security to investors that not only would the film be completed but there was a good chance of securing a return. Many low-budget independent British films stumble at this early stage due to a lack of confidence from possible investors and distributors, even when filmmakers have a proven track record.

A complicating factor to scheduling production was the availability of Jones' preferred lead actor, Sam Rockwell. Increasingly in demand throughout the first decade of the twenty-first century, Rockwell was shooting and too busy at that point to read Parker's second draft script for *Moon*. Shooting had been scheduled to begin in January 2008 to suit Rockwell's schedule, but while Fenegan was raising finance, the movie was officially without a star name. To pressure Rockwell, Fenegan sounded out British actor Paddy Considine about playing Sam Bell, and let Rockwell's agent know. Within three days, Rockwell was confirmed for *Moon*. One of Rockwell's requirements was the ability to workshop the script. Jones spent a week in New York with Rockwell and his actor friend Yul Vasquez working their way through the script and revising where needed, incorporating some of the actors' ad-lib moments. Jones rewrote some of Parker's dialogue to better suit Rockwell, while Rockwell began the process of getting to grips with differentiating between the essentially exactly alike versions of Sam Bell. A month later Jones had a final shooting script.

The second most expensive item for the production (after Rockwell's fee) was the cost of building the moon base set at Shepperton. Construction was underway to meet the planned shooting schedule and the availability of Rockwell in early 2008, but without the confirmed funds that would flow from a distribution deal. Production designer Tony Noble designed a fully realised moon base set with no doubling of redressed components or tricking out sets as more than one location. This was an approach that Ridley Scott had adopted for the ship interiors featured in *Alien*, also filmed at Shepperton 30 years earlier. Gavin Rothery had already done much of the preparatory work, even creating computer generated images of several of the main interiors that would be the lunar home to Sam Bell. He also devised an animated 3D 'walkthrough' of the interior to give an indication of how the various rooms related to one another. Jones' other advertising colleague, Hideki Arichi, served as art director illustrating key concepts for the corporate and largely functional facility.

Movies in which a single actor plays one or more roles have a long history – Peter Sellers was notorious for disguising himself in various parts in a single film, perhaps most notably in Kubrick's *Dr. Strangelove* (1964); similarly Alec Guinness had depicted the entire nine-member D'Ascgoyne family in 1949's *Kind Hearts and Coronets*. Most often, actors have played direct doubles in films ranging from Charlie Chaplin in *The Great Dictator* (1940) to Richard Ayoade's adaptation of Dostoyevsky's novella *The Double* (2013). Most often, such characters are twins, as in *The Dark Mirror* (1946), featuring Olivia de Havilland, or *Dead Ringer* (1964), with Bette Davis. The most notable film of this type, and one consulted by Duncan Jones in preparing for *Moon*, was David Cronenberg's 1988 *Dead Ringers* starring Jeremy Irons as identical twin gynaecologists.

To achieve the scenes in which Sam Rockwell was to be acting against himself, portions of the movie had to be shot twice over. The production hired Rockwell lookalike Robin Chalk to interact with the star. They would film each scene twice, swapping roles (as well as make-up and costume) to film the other half. Chalk's performance would be entirely eliminated as scenes were composited to feature two Rockwells, but his presence was a technical necessity as well as necessary to Rockwell's pursuit of his performances as the various Sam Bells.

A WGA writers' strike that started in November 2007 and ran until February 2008 benefited the production of *Moon* in unexpected ways. As Jones was not yet a WGA member, *Moon* was able to continue shooting while many surrounding productions then filming at Shepperton were forced to close down, including Ridley Scott's *Robin Hood* (2010) with Russell Crowe and Universal's *The Wolfman* (2010) with Benicio del Toro. That freed up some stage space and Shepperton employees or associated on-site independent companies to work on *Moon*. Fenegan acquired access to unused Shepperton stages, allowing him to erect additional sets for the Bell family home and the Lunar Industries conference room. The cabin of Sam Bell's moon rover cab was able to be built upon a moveable gimbal rather than being squeezed into a corner of Shepperton's expansive K-stage which was now packed with the lunar base sets for *Moon*.

The sequences set away from the moon briefly featured additional cast members, such as Dominique McElligott as Sam's wife Tess, Rosie Shaw as his baby daughter Eve, Kaya Scodelario as the teenage Eve, and the pairing of Benedict Wong and Matt Berry as the Lunar Industries officials Thompson and Overmeyers. All these scenes were depicted on screens or as dream sequences, which is why it was hoped they could be achieved through smaller, more compromised set sections jerry-rigged on K-stage. The shut-down of those other productions, though, allowed *Moon* to expand and so become a more ambitious, more polished production.

The shoot for *Moon* comprised just over thirty days of main filming, a single day for pick-up shots by the main unit, and a further week for the miniature shoot with the moon surface, rover vehicles, and assorted lunar locations (for a total shoot of about 41 days). So tight was the budget that set dressing materials were sourced from the unlikeliest of places, including local hardware stores, takeaway shops, and even from crew members' homes. Some of Sam Bell's attire is, in fact, Sam Rockwell's own real-life clothing, including his 'Wake Me When It's Quitting Time' T-shirt, his tracksuit, and Hawaiian shirt. There was no room in the schedule for delay. The budget didn't allow for the traditional multiple sets of clothing for the lead – everything had to be kept in screen-ready condition, or immediately repaired if damaged. Through all this, Rockwell was tasked with keeping track of the mental states and various stages of decay of his Sam clones.

Following the intensive live action shoot was an equally pressured week of miniature filming. Digital effects were deemed to be unaffordable for the budget-minded production, so the fallback was an 'old fashioned' miniature shoot. In fact, contrary to popular belief miniatures continue to be employed in all kinds of filmmaking in conjunction with CGI effects. Much as *Star Wars: Episode I – The Phantom Menace* (1999) is often cited as one of the most CGI-intensive films made to that point, pioneering work on virtual set extensions, it is also true that the production was also one of the largest independent miniature shoots. *Star Wars* creator George Lucas pioneered motion control filming with miniature spacecraft in the original *Star Wars* (1977) and continued to do so throughout his productions. If it was good enough for Lucas, it was good enough for Duncan Jones.

There were a variety of vehicles and lunar landscapes to be achieved through this method, including the automated Helium-3 harvesters, the moon rovers driven by Sam, the exterior of the Lunar Industries facility, and the signal-blocking towers that cut off communications between Earth and the moon. The production hired experienced movie model maker Bill Pearson to run the *Moon* miniature model shop, which was handy as he and his team were based at Shepperton Studios. Pearson had model credits on such productions as *Alien*, *Flash Gordon* (1980), *Outland*, and more recent productions such as Daniel Craig's debut as James Bond, *Casino Royale* (2006). Pearson was on the verge of retirement and intent on closing down his model shop, but he was persuaded to delay that after reading the script for *Moon*.

Unexpectedly, Pearson's model team also found themselves given the responsibility for the on-set realisations of Gerty, Sam Bell's HAL-9000 style robotic assistant. The roots of Gerty lay in the Carling C2 commercial that Jones shot in 2007. Jones dubbed a pair of robots in the ad as 'Gerty's mummy and daddy', highlighting a robot suspended from a rail embedded in the ceiling and another droid composed of old PC and Mac computers. Boxy and with limited mobility, the 'Gerty 3000 Robotic Assist' echoed such 1970s robotic helpers as the trio of helpful diminutive droids in *Silent Running*, and characters like V.I.N.C.E.N.T., Old B.O.B, and Maximilian from Disney's *The Black Hole* (1979). Like Gerty, these digital devices were infused with a sense of an almost human personality. It was to another ad he'd made that Jones turned when looking for the voice for Gerty, hiring Kevin Spacey who'd appeared in his Olympus camera commercial.

Although much of the specifics of Gerty would be finessed in post-production through CGI, it was necessary to have a practical prop that was as near-functional as possible on set for the benefit of Rockwell, who when he wasn't interacting with himself was involved in conversations with Gerty. The idea of Gerty partially communicating mood through digital emoticons was later lifted by the *Doctor Who* episode 'Smile' (2017), with Peter Capaldi's Doctor encountering several 'emojibots'.

Even with the extensive model work, and on a limited budget, *Moon* still had to employ a certain amount of CGI-related trickery in post-production to seal the deal in making the lunar world of Sam Bell entirely believable. The visual effects by Cinesite were employed in post-production to add to the verisimilitude of the lunar and industrial environments. Cinesite, who previously worked on several of the *Harry Potter*, *Marvel* superhero, and *Pirates of the Caribbean* movies, had to complete about 300 visual effects shots on a very limited budget and tight timescale.

The bulk of the visual effects work involved blending the two performances from Rockwell as Sam Bell 1 and Sam Bell 2 into convincing single scenes. These ranged from simple-to-realise split screen shots through to complex sequences like the ping-pong scene or the physical altercation between the two Sams. Although intended to be seamless and virtually invisible, the role of visual effects was key in achieving the success of *Moon* in convincing viewers of the realism of Sam Bell's predicament, trapped on the moon with no one but himself.

Jones admits that his approach to making his first feature was 'ass backwards'. He said, 'We knew what the budget had to be before we knew what the film was going to be. [From my commercials work] I had a pretty good understanding of what effects would be the most cost-effective. We knew we wanted a controlled shooting environment so that meant we would want to shoot everything in a studio, if we could. That gave me a starting point for what the story should be.'[6]

Rather than set out to create a particular film, Jones and his team had created a film suitable to both their limited resources and their nascent abilities. Drawing upon his own life, as well as that of Rockwell, Jones created a character in Sam Bell that was ideally suited to a solo three-year tour of duty on the moon. What Bell was not prepared for was the discovery that he was not the 'original' Sam Bell, that instead of three years, he and his fellow five clones (of many, many more in hidden storage) had in fact been isolated on the lunar surface for a total of 15 years. The real Sam Bell was happily ensconced at home with his now-teenage daughter.

It was a deliberate policy on behalf of Jones to return to a kind of cerebral science fiction that was somewhat out-of-vogue in the blockbuster era of the twenty-first century but that had been the preserve of low-budget filmmaking for many years. 'A lot of science-fiction films these days are a string of special-effects set pieces,' complained Jones. 'I miss those science fiction films which focused on people and storytelling, explaining how a human being survives and maintains their humanity in an alien environment or how their humanity is eroding away. Films like *Outland*, *Silent Running* and *Alien* did that. They were all about human beings and how they survived such scenarios. I wanted *Moon* to do that.'[7]

At the centre of *Moon* is not the lunar body itself, but that of the sole human inhabitant, Sam Bell. It is through Sam's experience that audiences are able to see the humanity that is denied by Lunar Industries in their cynical employment of human clones to help maximise their profits. Through Sam Bell *Moon* tackles questions of identity, isolation, industrial policy, human rights, as well as questions surrounding religion, work, and reward. The duplications of Sam Bell do not make him any less human. Just like the moon itself was explored by the astronauts of the Apollo programme, so the film *Moon* is a text that invites (and supports) detailed exploration by the curious viewer who can sense the depths contained beneath the lunar regolith.

Notes

1. '*Moon* is Duncan Jones' Homage to Classic Sci-Fi', *Wired* (12 June 2009) https://www.wired.com/2009/06/duncan-jones-moon/.
2. Caroline Graham, 'Zowie Bowie: How a son of rock royalty survived a bitter rift with his mother to earn genuine success'. *Mail on Sunday* (8 August 2009).
3. Simon Ward, *Making Moon: A British Sci Fi Cult Classic* (London: Titan Books, 2019).

4. Simon Ward, *Making Moon*.
5. Simon Ward, *Making Moon*.
6. Matthew Hutson, 'Duncan Jones on the Moon', *Psychology Today* (July 2009).
7. Steve Erickson, 'Director Duncan Jones on Low-Budget Moon', *Studio Daily* (June 2009).

Chapter Two: Isolation and Identity

One of the big questions that science fiction engages with is the definition of humanity. What makes a human being, in contrast to a robot AI (such as Gerty) or an artificial being (like the Sam clones), or even an alien life form (an area *Moon* does not explore, beyond Gerty's digital non-human intelligence)? This was an area that was fundamental to the science fiction of American author Philip K. Dick, whose work *Moon* director Duncan Jones was very familiar with.

Dick's writing spanned the end of the pulp era in the 1950s to the end of the 1960s 'new wave' in science fiction at the dawn of the 1980s. Dick died in 1982, aged just 53. Much of his work anticipated the genre of cyberpunk that came to dominate commercial science fiction in the 1980s, led primarily by William Gibson (*Neuromancer*, 1984), but Dick's most frequent thematic engagement was over questions of what defined a human being, often through questions of personal identity. Jones drew upon these explorations when devising the story for *Moon*.

The film presents artificial disposable bodies with a three-year lifespan. These are designated clones of the original Sarang moon-base contractor Sam Bell. While we are briefly shown what appears to be the original Sam Bell happily living out his domestic life on Earth, it is not clear if he actually served any time at the Lunar Industries facility or if he simply 'donated' his template to produce the clones (in promotional interviews around the release of the film, Jones suggested the original Sam Bell enjoyed a 'substantial pay day' in either case). Jones' film does not explore the backstory of how the cloning process works, when it was instigated, or how the decision to use a clone of a specific single human being was arrived at.

The three-year lifespan matches the period of service that 'Sam Bell' has supposedly contracted with Lunar Industries. As the film opens, we are presented with what we initially believe to be an authentic human being, serving out the end of his contract working alone (apart from 'robotic assist' Gerty) on the moon harvesting Helium-3 (He-3) to provide energy back on Earth. It is only because of the accident that occurs when Sam goes out onto the surface in a rover to investigate a malfunctioning He-3 harvester that the fact that he is not the 'original' Sam Bell is uncovered.

Without that accident, it can be assumed that the process would continue without interruption. When Sam uncovers the stash of further clones, the red lines on the storage units indicate five have been used (given their three-year lifespan, that suggests at least 15 years). There are row upon row of further clones awaiting future activation (it is suggested in Jones' follow-up and tangentially related film *Mute*, 2018, that there are 160 stored clones in total). Lunar Industries were clearly prepared for the process of activating and disposing of Sam clones to go on for some time (the three-year lifespan suggests a possible duration for the project of 480 years!). With the help of Gerty, the older of the two Sam clones uncovers a series of video logs that indicate each of the past clones has deteriorated towards the end of their three years' service. Each previous Sam is shown embarking upon what they believe to be the return journey to Earth by boarding a capsule, but this is revealed to be an incinerator that simply disposes of the 'old' Sam before the system activates another clone.

It may be that the three-year lifespan is a built-in fault of the cloning process, that the cloned bodies can only survive that long. Alternatively, the clones may be constructed with a built-in genetic trigger that results in the physical deterioration at the three-year point (in promotional interviews Jones suggested this limit was more 'sociological', as he believed it was about how long someone could exist in isolation). The idea of a limited lifespan in an artificial 'human' echoes Ridley Scott's *Blade Runner*, based upon Philip K. Dick's novel *Do Androids Dream of Electric Sheep?* (1968). In that movie, the 'replicants' (simply 'androids' in Dick's novel), that have been created to carry out dangerous or tedious tasks on the off-world colonies, have a built-in four-year lifespan. The replicants are copies of human beings, lacking only one aspect – genuine emotion. They are, however, equipped with artificial memories (those of Sean Young's replicant Rachael are drawn from replicant creator Tyrell's own niece), necessary to maintain their sanity. The development of possible 'emotional responses' (detected through the Voight-Kampff empathy test) in the Nexus-6 model of replicant was, according to Captain Bryant (M. Emmet Walsh), the reason that the Tyrell Corporation instituted the four-year lifespan. The escaped replicants that return to Earth, led by Rutger Hauer's Roy Batty (Baty in the original novel), seek their creator Eldon Tyrell (Joe Turkel) in order to extend their existence, which Tyrell argues has proven to be impossible.

Scott and screenwriters Hampton Fancher and David Peoples' expansion of Dick's original work was a clear influence on Jones and Nathan Parker in devising the story of *Moon*. Unlike the replicants of *Blade Runner*, the clones in *Moon* do not appear to benefit from any enhancements, such as superior strength or endurance. They are merely intended to be 'human' supervisors of the largely automated Helium-3 harvesting process. Neither do the Sam clones require artificial memories – the memories that Sam experiences appear to be genuine, even if they are some 15 years out of date. They are built upon by each Sam Bell clone's unique experiences.

Despite these superficial differences, Jones' creation of Sam Bell and Philip K. Dick's definition of what makes a human being, and differentiates him from an artificial being, 'android', or clone, share much. At the root of humanity, both texts argue, is empathy – an understanding of and sympathetic feeling toward and with other human beings. The Voight-Kampff test in *Blade Runner* specifically detects empathy, and therefore the emergence of true emotion or 'humanity' in the artificial replicant lifeforms. In *Moon*, the two Sams have empathy towards one another, as well as for their absent wife and child left behind on Earth. In this respect, they are true copies of the original Sam Bell, secure in their belief that their emotions are 'real'. Concern for the lives of others, even if that 'other' is another version of yourself, is deemed proof or reassurance of an inherent humanity.

Similarly, through the Sam Bell clones, *Moon* explores the question of a human as the sum totality of all their memories and experiences. As with *Blade Runner* and Dick's source novel, through the clones *Moon* explores the veracity of memory. If the memories of the Sam clones are not really theirs (inherited from the original template Sam Bell), in what way can they be said to have lived, to have an individual personality, to be, in fact, truly human? Presumably, across each three-year lifespan each clone accrues additional new, individually diverse memories, thus differentiating between the clones (although it does appear that, simply due to the nature of the routine work required, they probably fall into similar repeated patterns of existence; perhaps this way of life also makes them something less than human, too?). Identity can be created (or re-created), but can never be consistently maintained – each iteration of Sam Bell will – perhaps superficially, perhaps more profoundly – deviate from those that came before and those that come after.

Several recent science-fiction and horror movies have explored isolation or featured a single protagonist who has to fend for themselves. The 2007 version of *I Am Legend* (the third adaptation of Richard Matheson's 1954 novel) saw US Army virologist Robert Neville (Will Smith), as the apparent last man on Earth, battle zombie hordes. *Oblivion* (2013) features Tom Cruise as one of the last custodians of the planet Earth, who uncovers a secret history with connections to that of Sam Bell. In *Gravity* (2013), much of the film follows the plight of astronaut Dr. Ryan Stone (Sandra Bullock) who must make her way from her destroyed Space Shuttle to the International Space Station before a threatening cloud of space debris completes an orbit of the Earth and strikes again. *The Martian* (2015) saw Matt Damon's astronaut Mark Watney left behind on the red planet Mars where he has to survive by himself while awaiting rescue. While he's not strictly alone in that his wife and son are with him, in *The Shining* (1980) Jack Nicholson's Jack Torrance is very much the psychological focus of the movie. Other characters are in a form of self exile: Dr. Manhattan (*Watchmen*, 2009) and Yoda (*Star Wars: Episode V – The Empire Strikes Back*, 1980). The 1975 film *A Boy and his Dog* (based upon a cycle of stories by Harlan Ellison) sees Vic (Don Johnson) traversing a post-apocalyptic Earth with only his telepathic dog, Blood, for company. Other non-genre works featuring similar solo protagonists include Tom Hanks in *Cast Away* (2000), Ryan Reynolds in *Buried* (2010), and James Franco in *127 Hours* (2010).

As we are introduced to Sam Bell in *Moon*, we believe (as he does) that he's a working class stiff coming to the end of a period of employment. The real-world equivalent might suggest oil-rig workers, who spend months at a time separated from friends and family while they work off-shore, often earning higher sums of money in a shorter period of time than they might otherwise (this is partly seen as compensation for this separation, but also a recognition of the potential dangers involved). Given Bell's isolation, though, the life of a Victorian- or Edwardian-era lighthouse keeper might be a more suitable analogy. Often dispatched in pairs to geographically isolated locations to maintain the lights that warn ships away from danger, lighthouse keepers can experience many of the side-effects of isolation, especially in terms of disintegrating identity (as explored in the 2019 movie *The Lighthouse*, co-written and directed by Robert Eggers).

The first Sam Bell we meet is later revealed to be Clone #5, while the one awakened later in the film and who escapes to Earth at the climax is Clone #6 (following the filmmakers' example, these individuals will be designated Sam 1 and Sam 2 in this text). It is through uncovering his own true history that Sam begins to deconstruct his identity. There are early indications that three years of effective solitary isolation (apart from the non-human Gerty) are getting to Sam. Unable to contact Earth in real-time (an artificially induced state of affairs to maintain the deception that Sam has only been on the moon for three years; communication is limited to a repeating library of pre-recorded videos), Sam has been without genuine human contact for the entire period of his stay.

One of the effects of long-term isolation, determined through studies with solitary confinement prisoners, is that people become prone to hallucinations and degradations in their conceptual capacity. Such isolation makes humans prone to '… perceptual distortions and hallucinations, affective disturbances, difficulty with thinking, memory and concentration difficulties, disturbances of thought content, and problems with impulse control'.[1]

Sam 1 begins to suffer hallucinations. The first substantial one is a woman sitting in his favourite armchair, and the second is an indistinct figure on the surface of the moon that causes him to crash his rover into the harvester. It is only later in the film that it becomes clear that these hallucinations are of his by-now teenage daughter, Eve. Given that this clone is only three years old and has inherited the original Sam Bell's memories, he still believes his daughter to be around three years of age. How, therefore, does the Sam clone have the awareness to hallucinate his daughter at her current age, something he is supposed to be unaware of?

Duncan Jones tackled this question in a number of interviews following the release of the movie as it became a point of conversation. '*Moon* is intended to be a hard science fiction film, which means we try to build and extrapolate on present day science,' said Jones. 'Occasionally, we start to touch into soft science fiction, which is more fantastical. But, I still argue that there is a roughly scientific idea behind it. You hear stories of identical twins when they're separated, sensing or having a feeling or awareness of anything major or traumatic that happens to their identical twin, even if they're not in contact. So, the idea is that Sam on the base is able to sense and feel that there exists a daughter, a girl, which is the daughter of the original Sam back on Earth. That's how they're all connected and that's why Sam's having these visions. Because, basically, this girl means so much to the original Sam.'[2]

Another aspect of Sam's 'difficulty with thinking, memory and concentration difficulties' is revealed in his relationship with his plants – he converses with them as if they are people. The *Moon* screenplay refers to the 'greenhouse' as 'a dark storage area Sam has repurposed to grow a handful of plants. They sit surrounded by darkness, glowing under pools of artificial light'. In a witty touch, each of the plants is given a name (visibly written upon their egg box-like plant pots). They are all named after prominent science-fiction filmmakers that Jones admires, among them Stanley (Kubrick), George (Lucas), Ridley (Scott), Kathryn (Bigelow), and Stephen (Steven Spielberg). Sam plays classical music to the plants, as much to soothe himself as to soothe them. He is projecting onto the plants the factor that is missing from his life on the moon: fellow human beings to converse with. Sam has co-opted his plants as alternative people, given them names, and happily relates his mood and accounts of his activities to them as if they could hear him and understand. In a way, he can relate to the plants better than he can to Gerty (who does talk and can understand him and respond to him, but is programmed to do so) as they are organic, like him.

Similarly, Sam as we first meet him has a single overriding focus: he wants to return home. The closer he comes to what he perceives as the end of his three-year term, the more anxious he becomes to be back on Earth with his family. This is again accounted for in real-life studies of individuals who are deliberately isolated (again, prison populations tend to be the basis for these psychological investigations). This can manifest in '…a kind of "tunnel vision" in which … attention becomes stuck … [and one] cannot stop thinking about the matter; instead … [one] … becomes obsessively fixated upon it'.[3] The 'matter' in question here is Sam's imminent return home: it is a prospect that comes to dominate his waking thoughts, infiltrates his dreams, and informs his reactions when he finds out the truth about his own nature and his unusual predicament.

The fundamental reason that Sam is so keen to return home is so he can resume family, community, and human contact. That, being a three-year-old clone, he has never actually experienced any of these things 'for real' makes no difference – within Sam's construction of his 'self', he has a wife, a child, and presumably a wider social circle back on Earth. He is utterly unaware that his cognisance of these things is at least 15 years out-of-date. Life on Earth has moved on without him: his wife, Tess, is now dead (we're never told how this has come about), and his daughter, Eve, is a near-adult teenager. He has been frozen in time, a facsimile of the man that the original Sam Bell was a decade and a half earlier.

The notion of the 'self' does not develop in isolation. The Sam Bell clones arrived as fully formed adults, complete with memories and experiences they perceive as having been 'lived'. However, the self can only be defined in opposition or in contrast to other similar human beings – growing up, people develop their own character through their experiences and the influence of the other (older, adult) humans around them, whether that be within their family (the primary source of such socialisation) or in wider peer groups, such as the local community, schools, or, ultimately, work places. The Sam clones have been denied this 'natural' socialisation, instead piggy-backing on the implanted memories of an unacknowledged 'other'. The construction of human identity relies upon such successful socialisation. Each of the Sam Bell clones is 'born' fully formed, having inherited someone else's past socialisation. Does that make them the 'same' as the original Sam Bell? After they divert, in behaviour and in the creation of new memories, can the clones still be said to be 'Sam Bell' at all? He is a clone of an absent original: real life is going on elsewhere.

As postulated by French psychoanalyst Jacques Lacan, the 'mirror stage'[4] in human development occurs at about the age of six months, by which point a normally developing human child recognises their existence from outwith themselves (normally suggested by response to seeing a reflection of themselves in a mirror). Since Lacan first suggested this in 1949, there has been some debate about the literalness of interpretation as to whether an actual mirror is required or not. Either way, the theory stands – at some point, the human consciousness recognises its own physicality within the human body as separate from 'itself'. The mirror element is essentially a metaphor for the ability of a human being to recognise itself from outside itself.

Individual people's perceptions of themselves (in actual mirrors or in the abstract) is often entirely subjective and can be in stark contrast to objective reality. Some forms of mental illness can be seen as the result of such psychological misperceptions of the individual human body, such as body dysmorphic disorder in which there is a persistent and intrusive preoccupation with an imagined or slight defect in a person's physical appearance. Such concerns can cause severe emotional distress and difficulties in daily functioning. This can in turn lead to such secondary eating disorders, such as Bulimia Nervosa, Anorexia Nervosa, Binge Eating Disorder, or various forms of self-harm.

Until he is confronted with the second Sam, Sam 1 is otherwise happy enough in his identity and his sense of self, even if his long-term isolation is beginning to get to him, thus provoking his urgent desire to return home. There is an immediate distinction between the two Sams, beyond the injury to Sam 1's hand that he sustained when he was distracted by his 'vision' of Eve, his teenage daughter. The first Sam the viewer meets has, in contrast to the newer arrival, developed a more mellow outlook. He is more or less happy with his lot, although the end of his contract (two weeks away) is ramping up his desire to reunite with his distant family. He presumably began in the exact same mental and behavioural place as the 'new' Sam 2, but has over time cultivated a more reflective, peaceable persona, where he is happy to listen to classical music and chat amiably with the plants he lovingly cultivates. He has spent much of his three years constructing a detailed model village, an activity that Parker's screenplay describes as 'difficult and complicated work' that 'over three years Sam has become highly skilled at'. It's a model of Sam Bell's home town of Fairfield, where his family – Tess and Eve – live. He has even carved detailed individual models of them among the other townspeople. The dedication involved in building such a detailed model suggests that this Sam has got over the impatience and anger issues displayed by the new, less developed Sam. As Sam 2 (as designated in the screenplay) admits after their physical fight: 'I've got a temper. I need to do something about it.' Sam 1 has already tackled this issue.

The cause of the fight is the very same model, which Sam 2 destroys in his search for a hidden clone store in the moon base. Sam 2 asked how long it had taken to construct, provoking the response from Sam 1: 'I don't remember doing all of it. I remember when I did the church and the Salvation Army. And a few of the people. My mind's been acting kind of weird lately, though.' Gerty later confirms that Sam has spent 938 hours on the model (that could work out at an hour or so for each day of Sam's three-year tenure). Gerty also confirms the status of Sam's experiences of life before being awakened: 'They are memory implants., Sam. I'm very sorry.'

The question of Sam 2's apparent short temper is an immediate marker of difference between the clones, an illustration of how living life on the moon, tackling the assigned daily tasks, changes the initial clone in some fundamental aspects of its nature. Sam 1 is clearly calmer and more together than his 'replacement'. Before Sam 2 arrives, Parker's screenplay highlights various points where Sam 1 has to work at controlling his temper, notably when he is recording a message for his superiors back on Earth where he begins to get annoyed at the lack of real-time communication. He recognises this trait is full-blown in the new Sam, and complains to Gerty about it. This allows Sam 1 some self-reflection, a recognition of how he has progressed as a person over his three years of isolation. Gerty asks Sam 1 what it is about Sam 2 that scares him. 'He flies off the handle. I see it now ... I see what Tess was talking about.' Sam recognises that Tess left him for six months the year before he came to the moon because of his short temper. He continues: 'She gave me a second chance. I'd promise her I'd change.' Gerty confirms that Sam has changed, and he agrees.

This change in Sam, this self-development, has come about during his isolation. The biggest changes, however, come when Sam is confronted by himself. Sam 2 has not yet embarked upon that process of change. As far as he is concerned, he is newly arrived on the moon (or, as a clone, newly 'born'): he remains the short-tempered, hot-headed, aggressive Sam Bell that almost drove Tess away. He has not had the time in isolation to reflect upon his own nature and so work at becoming a better human being. This is a spin on Lacan's 'mirror stage': the Sams are confronted with each other, and so begin to have an effect on one another. They begin to change together in unexpected ways after being confronted with their true 'selves'. Their isolation from both Earth and humanity leads to the asking of existential questions.

The nearest we have currently to clones are human twins. Twins, even identical twins, can grow up to become radically different individuals as adults. In contrast, some remain remarkably similar in their tastes, occupations, and outlooks, even when separated by time or space (as is shown in cases of twins separated at or soon after birth who grow up to be similar people despite very different backgrounds). The clones in *Moon* are purely utilitarian. They are functional, have a simple job to do (supervising the process of mining of Helium-3 and dispatching it to Earth), and are apparently not given a second thought as actual 'human beings' by the company that created or employs them, Lunar Industries. In the worst meaning of the terms, the Sam Bell clones are no more than 'human resources' to be used and then disposed of when they have reached their term limits. They appear to have no 'human rights' as such might be recognised back on Earth.

Two decades into the twenty-first century, human cloning (defined as producing genetically identical copies of an organism) appears to be technically possible, but it remains ethically questionable and is currently banned. *Moon* posits a near future where this reservation seems not to apply, and cloning has been adopted to provide a solution to a problem. The clones of Sam Bell are the same age as the original human was when copied. Unlike the most widely known result of real-world cloning, Dolly the sheep (1996–2003), the Sam Bell clones are not grown from infancy. They appear to arrive fully formed as adults (at least, that's what we see in the hidden clone storage facility). The fantasy aspect of this is that these clones are 'awakened' as adults already imbued with Sam Bell's complete memories, including his awareness of his wife and daughter (which raises the associated question: why did Lunar Industries not chose someone with no emotional ties at home on Earth for their clone template?).

As environmental factors cause the lives of even identical twins to diverge, so the different day-to-day experiences of each of the five revived Sam Bell clones must produce slightly different Sam Bells at the end of each three-year term of duty. Genetics and identity are not so fundamentally connected as most people might reasonably assume.

In science-fiction literature and films, clones are a familiar concept. Sometimes they are the result of technology, as in the replication of an individual through matter duplication (the 1966 *Star Trek* episode 'The Enemy Within' is a classic of the type, as William Shatner's Captain Kirk is split into two psychologically incomplete individuals – one 'evil', one 'good' – due to an accident with the ship's matter transporter). From such 1930s works as William F. Temple's *Four-Sided Triangle* (1939, later filmed by Hammer Films in 1953), to Ira Levin's *The Boys From Brazil* (1976, filmed in 1978), the concept of cloning has been heavily explored in science-fiction literature and movies. Authors as diverse as Richard Cowper (*Clone*, 1972), Norman Spinrad (*The Iron Dream*, 1972), Arthur C. Clarke (*Imperial Earth*, 1975), and Ben Bova (*The Multiple Man*, 1976), have explored human cloning in the context of the science-fiction action-adventure narrative.

In movies, cloning was used to revive the dinosaurs in the *Jurassic Park* series (1993–present), and has been explored in such populist movies as *Alien: Resurrection* (1997), *The 6th Day* (2000, which duplicated Arnold Schwarzenegger), and *Star Wars: Episode II – Attack of the Clones* (2002), which revealed that the Stormtrooper army were all clones sourced from a single individual, Jango Fett (Temuera Morrison). The use of clones in film has ranged from comedy (*Multiplicity*, 1996; Jones purposely avoided this movie as he didn't see it as relevant to his approach) to heartfelt YA drama (*Never Let Me Go*, 2010, based upon the 2005 Kazuo Ishiguro novel; the notion of clones as a source for 'spare parts' in organ transplants was further explored in Michael Marshall Smith's novel *Spares*, 1996, and the film *The Island*, 2005). Perhaps the most obvious echo of the Sam Bell character is Jack Harper (Tom Cruise) in *Oblivion* (2013). In the year 2077, Harper believes himself to be one of the last humans alive following a conflict with the alien Tet; his functionary role is to repair combat drones. He is eventually revealed to be a Tet-controlled clone, Tech 49, implanted with false memories, a discovery that drives him 'off mission'.

The question the existence of the Sam Bell clones raises is do they enjoy any 'human' rights? Do these functional clones deserve categorisation as human beings, or does their limited role and lifespan, as well as their artificial nature, make them something else? As far as the Sam Bell viewers first meet in *Moon* is concerned, he's a simple human, the same as anyone else, the same as his wife and child on Earth, and the same as the pair of Lunar Industries representatives he receives video messages from. Until the accident with the rover and the He-3 harvester, he has little reason to believe otherwise (although those troubling hallucinations are beginning to bother him). When the next Sam in line is activated, he is in a similar position, until he discovers his predecessor injured in the crashed rover.

It appears that Lunar Industries has no contingency plan to deal with this kind of situation, and presumably at least 15 years into the programme they had no need of one; the hand-over from one Sam to another (supervised by Gerty) has always gone smoothly, with one being incinerated and a new version being awoken in his place. As far as Lunar Industries are concerned, the clones are simply another utility or tool, like the rovers or the harvesters. They're not regarded as humans with employment rights. In fact, Sam 2 comes to believe that the 'rescue' team sent to help them is in fact an 'assassination squad' sent to terminate their existence as part of a Lunar Industries cover-up.

This puts the Sam Bell clones in the same category as Gerty and as Philip K. Dick's androids or *Blade Runner*'s replicants: they have been created to do a singular job and have no recognised worth outside of that job (despite the scientific breakthrough implied by the creation of fully adult clones complete with intact human memories – what other uses could they be put to?). Does the clone of a single man – the original Sam Bell (who may or may not know that he has been the template for Lunar Industries' clones) – constitute a separate, distinct, and independent consciousness?

Lunar Industries go to a lot of effort to maintain the illusion that Sam is an independent human, complete with young family back on Earth. Their corporate representatives, Thompson (Benedict Wong) and Overmeyers (Matt Berry), are charged with sending Sam recorded messages in response to any issues he may raise. For Agustín Berti and Andrea Torrano, 'The videoconference between Lunar's directors (Thompson and Overmeyers) and Gerty makes evident the hierarchy of the robot over the clone.' This recalls the depiction of the hidden android in Ridley Scott's *Alien* (1979), Ash (Ian Holm), and his secret agenda.[5] A steady diet of pre-recorded video messages from Sam's wife Tess (Dominique McElligott) are supplied, as are recordings of 'recent' football matches (Sam says: 'I just wanted to thank you for sending out the football feed. Almost felt live!'). They are also maintaining the fiction that 'live' real-time contact with Earth is not possible due to a satellite malfunction, hence the need for pre-recorded communications. Lunar Industries are maintaining this fiction thanks to signal blocking towers surrounding the moon base, which Sam 2 later discovers. All of this could be argued to be a form of psychological torture of a kind that would surely be illegal if Sam Bell was considered to be a human being. In comparison to Gerty and the Sam clones 'men appear dehumanised: the managers of Lunar Industries, in their lust for profit, deceive the clones making them believe in their humanity, but show no concern for them other than the economic cost of the loss of a clone in the accident outside the base'.[6] The clones are, in fact, an extension of the moon base itself, just another tool for the generation of profit.

Scott Bukatman argues that 'the body has long been the repressed content of science fiction, as the genre obsessively substitutes the rational for the corporeal, and the technological for the organic'.[7] In *Moon*, Sam Bell's artificially cloned 'human' body is the space where various discourses concerning humanity and human rights are played out. If, as has been argued, the closer a machine (an android or replicant) resembles a human being, the more monstrously uncanny it becomes, where does that leave these virtually human clones?

There is no indication of the world of work outside Lunar Industries and Sam Bell's lonely existence in *Moon*, and no real indication of when this story might be taking place except for a vague concept of 'the near future'. The technology, vehicles, and equipment are all easily understood and do not appear too far advanced. Perhaps Gerty as a form of artificial intelligence, and Lunar Industries capacity to build a moon base and run an industrial operation on the surface of the moon, suggest the film could be set a few hundred years in the future at most. Certainly, the technology required to produce the viable and functional Sam Bell clones is currently fantasy.

There must be a reason why Lunar Industries would make an investment in the cloning programme to create and repeatedly re-create Sam Bell rather than training and sending human workers, as is currently done with oil rigs. The investment in the Sarang Mining Base is substantial, and much of it is dedicated to keeping Sam Bell alive and working. Why use clones, which seem to only be viable for a limited period of time, rather than robots? Would a fully automated mining base not be more cost effective, with occasional visits from human engineers to keep it running and make any repairs? Did Lunar Industries itself develop the cloning science that has produced the Sam Bell clones or did it originate elsewhere? It certainly appears from the ending (and in a scene in *Mute*) that the wider population of Earth, happily using the energy produced by the He-3 mined on the moon, are unaware of the sacrifices being repeatedly made by the Sam Bell clones in order to keep their lights on and their homes heated. It does not seem that the population of Earth as a whole has made a conscious, agreed ethical compromise to access cheaper energy; there is no suggestion that a climate crisis has led to an accommodation between the public and the authorities that the many deaths of Sam Bell is a price worth paying [see Chapter Three].

What *Moon* does suggest is that the corruption of corporations will, if anything, in the future be even worse than it appears to be now. From ethical violations to human rights abuses, corporations the world over have a poor record. When maximising profit is all that counts, the 'cost of business' is often reckoned in human lives. That's the course taken by Lunar Industries: whatever ethical compromise necessary to enact the cloning programme has already been entered into. The 'suffering' of each iteration of Sam Bell is taken into account as just another cost of doing business.

The benefit to Lunar Industries is that the 'three-year' contract need never end. It must be more cost-effective for Lunar Industries to utilise a series of blank Sams, suitably 'loaded' with the required memories and job-appropriate training and capabilities. The world of work, in the future envisioned in *Moon*, has been completely separated from the capabilities of the human body. There is no need for a 'genuine' human to run the risk of living and working on the moon when a seemingly endless supply of Sam Bell clones can do it instead. The human and the android are one-and-the-same.

Instead of the leap into the future that Stanley Kubrick imagined in the form of the 'star child' revealed at the climax of *2001: A Space Odyssey*, in *Moon* Jones envisions a copy of a single man as a representative of the inevitable dehumanisation of global (and lunar) capitalism. Sam Bell is not an explorer astronaut, like the crew of Kubrick's *Discovery One*, venturing into the unknown to solve a riddle (the receipt of a message from an alien intelligence). Instead, Sam is depicted as a working stiff, a working-class figure, an oil rig 'roughneck'. He works with huge machines that dwarf his human figure in the lonely lunar landscape. In fact, he is simply another piece of machinery, another asset, to be replaced when it breaks down and not given a second thought. Sam Bell is essentially a biological machine, a piece of equipment, no more no less. In the future of work envisioned in *Moon*, there is no place for the individual. It's an effective metaphor for the contemporary (and seemingly increasing) dehumanisation of the world of work in the early twenty-first century. Is a world where people are labelled 'human resources' or 'work units' any better than the future depicted in *Moon* in which artificially created 'human-like' work units (clones) carry out tasks that are difficult or dangerous?

Sam works within a brightly light, almost uniformly white environment – the kind of futuristic/industrial location that has been common in such films since Kubrick's *2001: A Space Odyssey*. While films like *Star Wars* (1977, more fantasy than science fiction) moved in the direction of a 'used universe', in which the worlds and technology appeared lived-in, films like *Moon* have a tendency to present pristine almost scientific environments within which humans work, distinct from their environment. Although seemingly clean, the spaces that Sam inhabits are also coldly technological – it is an anonymous environment which Sam has made some effort to personalise as the vintage pin-ups that decorate his sleeping area, or the smiley face 'emoticons' he uses to countdown to the imminent end of his three-year tour of duty, show.

There is a stark contrast between the promised clean, user-friendly environment that Sam inhabits and the ugly, dirty industrial process that the harvesters are engaged in. If at all possible, Sam stays away from the huge mining machines, and it is his journey to investigate a fault that leads to the ultimate revelation of his ongoing deception. The clean interiors of the moon base also contrast with the 'dirty' ethics involved in Lunar Industries decision to pursue human cloning as a solution to the Earth's energy problem. To the corporation, Sam is just another dispensable part of the system that supplies around 70 per cent of the Earth's energy needs.

In this respect *Moon* applies a look of the future evolved from the technology of today: if NASA were to build a moon base in the near future, it might look like the one in *Moon*. The film features a scientific background that could largely be described as 'plausible', one based in attention to scientific fact (crucially) at the time of writing the screenplay (such as the mining of He-3, which was once thought of as a cheap source of energy but has now been surpassed by the potential of cheaper, Earth-based, green energy like wind and wave power). For Katherine Springer, this positions *Moon* firmly within the realm of 'hard science fiction', a term originating in 1957 that denotes accuracy in science within a science-fiction story (as far as is possible).[8]

According to Scott Sundvall, Sam's artificial memories are also part of this corporate control of his existence: '... the use of artificial memory and inauthentic transmissions produce ideological conditioning and obedience – imaginary relations to otherwise real conditions – such can only work with the technologized micro-control of Sam Bell's movements (spatial control).' Sam Bell 2 'breaches the spatial parameters established for him'; control of the space Bell inhabits (the Sarang base, the moon itself) is important to corporate control. 'In order to control and reproduce Sam Bell's labour production, Lunar Industries had to conceal the clone production of Sam Bells (down below).' The constant replacement of these clones is an 'endless postponement' of his promised return home – 'instead of returning home, Sam Bell gets flushed away'.[9]

As an audience we are positioned by director and screenwriter to regard Sam Bell as a simple human attending to a series of routine tasks. This impression is reinforced by Sam Rockwell's performance before the fact of his cloning is revealed. He's an everyday 'Joe', who has exchanged his three years of labour for a (presumable) windfall payday that might mean he does not have to work again, or he can afford to buy outright a house for his wife and daughter. That's the bargain every 'worker' makes with capitalism: work for the money needed to purchase the quality of life desired. Instead, the Sam clones are condemned to a life of endless repetition as each iteration goes through the same process until he meets his fiery demise in the incinerator. A happy retirement is not on the cards for any version of Sam Bell.

The reality of Sam's day-to-day life and endless journey around what could be interpreted as a futuristic version of one of Dante's circles of Hell is in stark contrast to the utopian vision presented in the public relations film for Lunar Industries presented at the beginning of *Moon*. Later shots of a world able to take advantage of plentiful clean energy are contrasted with the opening shots of industrial pollution, landfill waste, and impoverished people. This short introduction serves a dual purpose: it sets up the world of *Moon*, succinctly explaining the nature of the He-3 mining project, and primes the audience to expect to follow the struggles of a lone individual as he attempts to maintain the system. Instead, the film goes on to question the role of the individual within this system, and whether there is a price too high to pay for bountiful energy. The film serves as a reminder of the human cost of such high-tech fixes for seemingly intractable human problems. For Berti and Torrano, however, this system is simply the fulfilment of the capitalist dream of 'production without labour force' where the Sam Bell clones exist as 'the manipulation and creation of a fictional life for corporative profit'.[10]

The question also has to be asked if human cloning is even a viable solution to work in such hostile environments as that of the moon's surface. Since the end of the United States' Apollo programme, which put man on the moon in 1969, human space exploration has consisted of near-Earth orbit manned missions (mainly to the International Space Station). Anything beyond Earth orbit has required unmanned space probes, robots, and rover vehicles. As of May 2021, there was a trio of operational Rovers on the surface of Mars: *Curiosity* and *Perseverance* (both US) and the *Zhurong* (China). Eight orbiters were surveying the planet and the stationary lander *InSight* (US) was investigating the deep interior. Further afield, deep space exploration has relied upon unmanned robotic probes, from *Luna 9* (Russian, 1966), the first man-made object to land on the moon, through various probes dispatched to the planets of the solar system (*Mariner 10*: Mercury; *Venus 7*: Venus), to those sent to study comets (*Stardust*; *Rosetta*), to deep space probes sent beyond our solar system (*Pioneer 10*; *Voyager 1* and *2*). All of this simply confirms that space – including the moon – is an environment currently deemed simply too hostile for humans to live and work in.

Robots are a solution to this, but the technology is not yet adequate to allow for a full moon base. Various plans have been suggested for a manned presence on the moon, or for mining of the asteroids, but any such scheme is currently a long way off. *Moon* posits Lunar Industries' human clones as a solution to the problems of manned space exploration (or exploitation). The mining of the moon would presumably be viable with a regularly rotating human crew of engineers, but Lunar Industries have deemed such an approach to be too costly in terms of their bottom line and shareholders' interests. Instead, the willing exploitation of a specially created 'near human' artificial being was seen as an ethically acceptable approach.

The prime example of technology that Sam Bell interacts with is Gerty, the 'robotic assist' supplied to help him maintain the base. For Springer, Gerty 'depicts the interface between humans and alien intelligence, including digital intelligence',[11] while Berti and Torrano see Gerty as underlying 'the issue of technologically manipulated biological organisms designed for labour exploitation'.[12] The character that Gerty most immediately calls to mind is not the friendly robots of *Star Wars*, like the humanoid C-3PO or dustbin-shaped R2-D2, but the much more malevolent HAL-9000 of *2001: A Space Odyssey*. Voiced with distant calm by Canadian actor Douglas Rain, HAL was a single red-eyed artificial intelligence intended to be an aide to the human astronauts aboard the *Discovery One*. Instead, the computer has been programmed with a counter-mission, and in its pursuit of that secret directive, the humans aboard are considered disposable, just like the Sam Bell clones.

According to Jones, Gerty has a singular focus: 'He's there to look after Sam and make sure that he survives for three years. That's it.'[13] However, in our first introduction to Gerty actor Kevin Spacey gives the character similar ominous-sounding tones to HAL, despite the mitigation of the human-like smiley faces on Gerty's interface. These are ersatz 'emotions', not real feelings – they are signifiers of emotions, symbols instead of feelings. Gerty has total control over Sam's environment, and the fear generated in the audience is that the film might pit man against machine in a battle for survival (again, echoing HAL in *2001: A Space Odyssey*). Instead, the opposite happens. Gerty follows through on its 'prime directive' to protect Sam, no matter how many of them there are.

For Robin Stoate, Gerty is significant in being the rare example of a non-hostile artificial intelligence in science-fiction film.

The non-anthropomorphic mode of embodiment taken by most AIs in fiction assigns them a particularly belligerent character. Unlike humanoid, more recognisably-embodied robots (such as C-3PO from the *Star Wars* series of films [1977–2005] or Commander Data from the television series *Star Trek: The Next Generation* [1987–1994]), these intelligent, self-aware subjects exist as free-floating essences, nevertheless bounded within the more recognisable, traditional shape of the immobile computer system – and they almost always seem to inspire a certain discomfort, or even outright paranoia [as in] computer-instantiated AIs such as HAL-9000 in *2001: A Space Odyssey* (1968), the Master Control Program of *TRON* (1982), [and] the WOPR war computer in *WarGames* (1983). ... The fact that these subjects lack a cohesive, visible body (and are, in many cases, seen to be omniscient through multiply-deployed camera 'eyes') is given as a constant source of fear.[14]

We're never given Gerty's point of view, unlike in the case of both HAL-9000 and the Terminator robot. It is left to emoticons to communicate Gerty's interiority.[15]

It is Gerty who fills in Sam on the backstory of the clones, allowing him access to his own history through video messages and mission logs, noting in a matter-of-fact style: 'It is standard procedure for all new clones to be given tests to establish mental stability and general physical health. Genetic abnormalities and minor duplication errors in the DNA can have considerable impact ...', before confirming that Sam's memories of Tess and Eve are 'memory implants'. When sending Sam 2 back to Earth, it is Gerty who volunteers an obvious flaw in the plan hatched by the two Sams. 'If the Rescue Unit examine my memory banks they will discover what has taken place over the last week. As you know I record everything. If they are suspicious, the first thing they will do is search my memory banks, and this would put you in considerable danger.'

Unlike HAL, Gerty follows through on protecting Sam even to the extent of volunteering for a memory wipe in order to preserve his secrets. For Berti and Torrano, Gerty never rebels against man (as HAL does), but assists Sam, bringing 'the machine closer to a living being'.[16] Where astronaut Dave Bowman had to physically deactivate HAL to prevent his interference by manually dismantling the computer's innards, Gerty instead offers a self-sacrificing, if practical, solution: 'I recommend erasing my memory banks. I can reboot myself once you have departed.' Any artificial intelligence Gerty may possess is limited – he has a programmed function and he follows it to the letter, even when it contravenes the wider interests of the corporation that created him. He is not 'sentient' in the way the Sam clones clearly are, but as Sam anthropomorphises Gerty – perhaps through loneliness, he needs someone 'friendly' to talk to – it seems as though Gerty is in fact manifesting a human-like consciousness or even conscience. Gerty's 'emotions' or 'moods' are simulated through the use of emoji-like smiley faces, but these cannot be taken as any true indication of replicant-like development of true emotions. According to Stoate, Gerty is the 'figure of the caring computer [that] represents a capacity for affective impact upon human subjects that is not normally ascribed to "emotionless" technological subjects … [*Moon* features] an unusual representation of care … as represented and embodied by interactions between a human clone and a computer'.[17] Gerty having a 'face' through these emoticons makes this process easier and therefore more convincing.

Gerty displays no outrage at the corporate machinations of Lunar Industries, as the two Sams do when they come to a clearer understanding of their predicament. While Gerty can fake something akin to embarrassment when caught having a seemingly real-time conversation with Earth, the computer shows no concern or even faked emotion about the fact that for a decade-and-a-half he has been happily replacing one Sam clone with another and continuing to serve as the corporation's factotum. The ethics of the situation are not programmed.

At the same time, Gerty is equally happy to help Sam 2 in his escape to Earth and to cover up for him as he departs. The computer makes no ethical judgment in either case: he is programmed to function as directed by Lunar Industries, and that primary direction appears to be to keep Sam safe and healthy. There is no contradiction in these seemingly mutually exclusive positions: Gerty simply 'does' as Gerty has been programmed to 'do', unlike the Sams who can use their innate 'human' intelligence to figure out their position and to react accordingly.

Jones knew what he was doing with his positioning of Gerty as initially a perceived possible antagonist to eventual 'friend' to the film's central character. '[Gerty] is actually a very simple machine with a very simple set of rules. But it's what we as an audience bring to it, assuming that it's gonna be like HAL, or it's what the Sams themselves bring to it, assuming it's their best buddy – that's really what matters.'[18] Ultimately, Gerty sacrifices his 'self' (his recorded memories) so Sam 2 can make real that which has only been artificial (his implanted memories).[19] Stoate notes that both Sam and Gerty are 'imprinted recipients of recorded memories, implanted to help maintain control over them', and similarly both are 'emblazoned with corporate branding – Gerty on his body and screen, the Sams in their clothes, almost all of which display the Lunar Industries' logo',[20] a brand of overt corporate ownership and inadvertent admission to their manipulation.

Sam Bell must be special – after all, an entire world-wide conspiracy revolves solely around him and his well-being (hence Gerty's mission to keep Sam 'safe' and to 'help' wherever possible).

Moon makes reference to films of the past but never itself descends into pastiche – the film is not a clone of something else more original. It instead remixes familiar elements into something new. The pull between originality and familiarity works to the movie's benefit. For example, the initial depiction of Gerty riffs off the audience's assumed cultural familiarity with the duplicitous HAL-9000 from Stanley Kubrick's *2001: A Space Odyssey*. This allows Parker and Jones to reveal Gerty as anything but the HAL model of malevolent AI, instead he 'helps' Sam whenever he can, even if that help would not be what his creator, Lunar Industries, would actually want him to be doing.

Through *Moon*, Duncan Jones demonstrates that identity is not programmed and that isolation cannot alone destroy the central core of a human being. The definition of humanity is explored, through the changing nature of the Sam Bell clones, through their contrast with the AI of Gerty (which can only offer 'performative' emotions), and through Sam's humanity in contrast to the inhumanity of the corporate practices of Lunar Industries. The nature versus nurture argument is explored, with each iteration of Sam Bell starting from identical points but varying across their three years of personal development. The yearning to return to his family posits the importance of such concepts as family, society, and human contact in maintaining human identity.

A dark future of work is explored through the questionable ethics of cloning, the lack of 'human' rights accorded to the clones, and the abuse of the clones by Lunar Industries.

Gerty's nature as the anti-HAL is in contrast to other such science-fiction movie artificial intelligences as Colossus (*The Forbin Project*, 1970), the Master Control Program (*TRON*, 1982), and SkyNet (*The Terminator*, 1984), all – just like Gerty – originally created to aid mankind, only to turn upon it. The 'unhuman' Gerty chooses between following its coding to help Sam and a directive to not let him outside, to maintain the secret of clones. As he leaves for Earth, Sam 2 removes a 'Kick Me' Post-It note stuck to Gerty's back as a joke. This is a recognition of Gerty's personhood from a clone who is now aware of his own nature. Sam 2 is inclined towards this view – that Gerty's reliance upon the ability to reason and evaluate based upon past experience, just as he does, signifies its essential humanity, as it is what he hopes for in his own case.

'People' is a more inclusive term than human, and comes to include Gerty – who is more 'human', the non-human clones or the non-human robotic assistant? The term 'human' is inadequate to the needs of 'people' like the Sam Bell clones or robot assist Gerty. Neither are passive objects of programming but are, in fact, people constituted by their own unique experiences and memories. Their bodies may be built, whether mechanically or genetically, but their minds are unique, even if they start off from base programming, as in Gerty's instructions or Sam's implanted memories.

Notes

1. Graham D. Glancy and Erin L. Murray, 'The Psychiatric Aspects Of Solitary Confinement', *Victims & Offenders* 1.4 (2006): 361-8.
2. Simon Brew, 'Duncan Jones Interview: The Man Who Made Moon', *Den of Geek* (November 2009) https://www.denofgeek.com/movies/duncan-jones-interview-the-man-who-made-moon/.
3. Stuart Grassian, 'Neuropsychiatric Effects Of Solitary Confinement. The trauma of psychological torture', PsycINFO (7 November 2012).
4. Jacques Lacan, 'The Mirror Stage as formative of the function of the I as revealed in

5. Agustín Berti and Andrea Torrano, 'Duncan Jones' Moon: Do clones dream of uncopyrighted sheep?', *Jura Gentium Cinema* (2012).
6. Ibid.
7. Scott Bukatman, *Terminal Identity: The Virtual Subject in Postmodern Science Fiction* (Durham, NC: Duke University Press, 1993).
8. Katherine Springer, 'Hard Science Fiction in Film: Analyzing Duncan Jones's Moon', *Film Matters* (Winter 2012).
9. Scott Sundvall, 'Clonetrolling the Future: Body, Space, and Ontology in Duncan Jones' *Moon* and Mark Romanek's *Never Let Me Go*', *Politics of Place*, 2 (16 March 2015).
10. Berti and Torrano, 'Do clones dream of uncopyrighted sheep?'
11. Katherine Springer, 'Hard Science Fiction in Film'.
12. Berti and Torrano, 'Do clones dream of uncopyrighted sheep?'
13. Erin McCarthy, 'Questions for Duncan Jones, Director of the Film Moon', *Popular Mechanics* (October 2009) https://www.popularmechanics.com/technology/gadgets/a4154/4313243/.
14. Robin Stoate, 'We're not programmed, we're people: Figuring the caring computer', *Feminist Theory* 13.2 (2012).
15. Berti and Torrano, 'Do clones dream of uncopyrighted sheep?'
16. Berti and Torrano, 'Do clones dream of uncopyrighted sheep?'
17. Robin Stoate, 'We're not programmed, we're people'.
18. '*Moon* is Duncan Jones' Homage'.
19. Berti and Torrano, 'Do clones dream of uncopyrighted sheep?'
20. Robin Stoate, 'We're not programmed, we're people'.

Chapter Three: The Look of the Future

The occupation of the moon appears to have been a peculiarly British concern, especially when it came to television (rather than film). While American science-fiction television productions of the 1960s and 1970s were exploring the far frontier in *Lost in Space* (1965–68), *Star Trek* (1966–69), and *Battlestar Galactica* (1978–79), British productions stuck closer to home with series set mainly or partially on the moon, such as *Moonbase 3* (1973), UFO (1970–71), and *Space 1999* (1975–77). Even *Star Cops* (1987) managed to spend a fair amount of time on the moon where the organisation's headquarters was located. American television has only produced two series of any significance directly concerned with the moon: the recent counter-factual alternate history of the space programme, *For All Mankind* (2019–present), and the acclaimed drama-documentary series *From the Earth to the Moon* (1998). All of these shows, American or British, faced the daunting prospect of designing the look of the future.

Similarly, design as an abstract element was important to *Moon* director Duncan Jones. As the son of David Bowie, a musician and artist for whom design (and repeated re-invention) was central to his various persona, Jones absorbed some of his father's attention to such seemingly abstract matters. It is almost as though Bowie's 1969 breakthrough single, 'Space Oddity', was a guiding force for Jones when it came to the visual aesthetic of *Moon*. The song – inspired both by Kubrick's *2001: A Space Odyssey* (1968) and the then-current Apollo 11 mission – was about an isolated man 'sitting in a tin can' and 'floating in a most peculiar way', according to the lyrics. Like Sam Rockwell's Sam Bell, Bowie's Major Tom is 'far above the world' where there is 'nothing [he] can do' to affect his basic situation. It is all in the hands of 'ground control', or Lunar Industries. Sam's yearning to be reunited with Tess is also covered: 'Tell my wife I love her very much, she knows'. There's even a hint of Gerty's role: 'I think my spaceship knows which way to go' and 'I think my spaceship knows what I must do', if read as suggestions of guidance by some form of AI.

Bowie revisited Major Tom over a decade later in 1980 with 'Ashes to Ashes'. Intended as an 'epitaph'[1] for his 1970s work and structured as a 'nursery rhyme', the song revises Major Tom's space voyage as a different kind of 'trip': 'We know Major

Tom's a junkie, strung out in Heaven's high, hitting an all-time low'. Bowie said of the song: 'It's about spacemen becoming junkies'.[2] That wasn't Bowie's final word on Major Tom, either. In 1995 he revisited the character one more time with 'Hello, Spaceboy'. The 'spaceboy' of the title is said to be 'so sleepy now' and 'so stationary' and is warned 'moon dust will cover you'. By the song's end, Spaceboy's identity is suggested in the lyric: 'Ground to Major, bye bye Tom, this chaos is killing me'. There's little Jones could do but absorb these influences, consciously or unconsciously. As a result, all of these specific Bowie song lyrics find echoes in the plot, characters, and design of Jones' *Moon*.

Jones, however, didn't face the task of designing *Moon* alone. His primary collaborator was Gavin Rothery, his visual design collaborator since their advertising days and their work on the short *Whistle* (2002). Rothery covered several areas on *Moon*, with his final credits encompassing conceptual design, graphic design, pre-vis (pre-visualisation) motion graphics, and visual effects supervisor. While Jones created the story and had the final say on all elements of design, Rothery was an important factor in determining the look of the moon base and everything in it, as well as that of the costumes, vehicles, and outposts on the moon's surface.

Writing on his website, Gavin Rothery outlined the initial approach to visualising *Moon*. 'I had free reign to come up with a moon base concept that we were actually going to build in its entirety. Duncan and I had been chatting general moon base stuff whilst getting the script together, so by the time I started the actual design process I'd already pretty much got it in my head.'[3] The basic approach was always to maximise the production value that could be achieved within the tight budgetary constraints the filmmakers were under. Responsibility for the look was divided between Jones, Rothery (who came up with most of the initial ideas between them), art director Hideki Arichi, and production designer Tony Noble, whose primary responsibility was to convert Rothery's 'conceptual' work into actual working designs that could be built within the physical confines of Shepperton Studios and the monetary confines of the budget.

Of all those involved with the look of *Moon*, Rothery was best placed to influence Jones – not only had the pair built a personal friendship together through their years working in advertising, but during the shooting of *Moon* Rothery and Jones shared a flat, an arrangement that had lasted the better part of a decade. Their sensibilities no doubt meshed to the extent that remembering who originated what might be difficult. While Jones had the overall production on his mind, Rothery was free, especially in the early days, to concentrate on developing their ideas for the visuals. It was Rothery who spent many hours developing computer-generated pre-visualisation images of the Sarang moon base, including a 3D 'fly-thru' of the interior of the base. While these visual aids were great tools for all involved, they did not get caught up in the detail of actual measurements – that was the focus of Tony Noble and construction manager Gene D'Cruze, who faced the task of turning the images from Rothery's digital world into something that could be built in the real world.

For Rothery, the early work on *Moon* originated within a domestic environment: '[It was] just me sitting in my bedroom knocking out designs and wandering through to the kitchen to chat about them with Duncan. The film came about basically through a couple of blokes wandering around their house drinking tea and talking about what we could do to make this film feel right.'[4] This domestic focus also helped to put the spotlight on the fact that the moon base was not only a functional industrial environment but also had to double up as Sam's home, the space where he lived, slept, and spent his off-duty leisure time. For each of the Sam Bell clones, the moon base was his entire universe. Rothery's position echoed the plight of the main character: 'Everything was pretty much made up as we went along. There was so much to do and I was on my own.'

Rothery's foundation was the need to make everything visible on *Moon* appear rooted in reality. The Sarang moon base had to look like a real facility; this wasn't the space fantasy of *Star Wars* or the far-future technology of *Star Trek*. The rule was that everything should, no matter how fantastic in concept, appear to be an extension of technology audiences would recognise from the actual early twenty-first century. Even if the film was set a hundred years from now (and the time period is left deliberately vague), Rothery's assumption was that most technology would still be largely recognisable, function encoded in form.

The other primary influence on *Moon*'s design aesthetic was all the other 'realistic' space films, largely of the 1970s, already mentioned (see Chapter One). Jones and his collaborators knew they simply did not have the budget of huge contemporary blockbusters such as *Transformers 2* (2009) or James Cameron's innovative *Avatar* (2009). Looking back to *Silent Running* (1972), *Logan's Run* (1976), and *Alien* (1979) gave Jones and Rothery a much more affordable aesthetic to emulate. The 'white' consumer goods look of the first two of those films and the industrial look of *Alien* were combined. 'I designed the film to make it look as if it was a lost film from the '70s or early '80s so that everything would fit together and the model work wouldn't look out of place,'[5] noted Rothery.

The overall aesthetic of the base interiors was designed to be cold and isolating, reflecting the plight of Sam Bell. The acres of white walls suggest high-end private BUPA hospitals where high-tech medicine is practised. Technology, in the form of screens and interfaces, is generally crammed into corners or nooks, leaving huge expanses of the wall space unadorned. Nothing is quite square, but neither are the shapes organic. The 'bays' appear as a receding set of cut out access spaces, where the edges are angled rather than curved. It is all very uninviting and not at all human. Little thought appears to have been given by Lunar Industries to the fact that a human being must exist within this environment for three years. 'The only thing Duncan really wanted was a main corridor that was kind of shaped like a key so I took this and incorporated a split-level roof,'[6] noted Rothery. 'The main corridor was designed first, then the airlock, infirmary, sleeping quarters, and finally the rec room [to the same shape].' This template for the corridors and the doors is not intrinsically human-orientated. It seems more suited to Gerty, who slides through the facility along a ceiling-based trackway, echoing each Sam Bell clone's largely predetermined route through life.

Rothery designed the entire moon base using 3D computer design programs and claims that little overall changed from his original concepts; the main compromises came in actually realising the physical dimensions of the sets and dressing them appropriately. Working within British domestic film production where money is tight, the crew of *Moon* had to make do with whatever they could lay their hands on. Originally intended to be located within a disused airlock, Sam's 'greenhouse' became a larger set when it was decided that more scenes would take place within it. This necessitated the creation of a new set that hadn't been budgeted for. The end result is an amorphous space without defined walls or edges, where Rockwell's character is hemmed in by spray-painted bread crates, tending to plants held in fast food containers. This kind of make-do approach extended to other examples of 'high-tech' future technology. The hair cutting machine used by Gerty to give the unkempt Sam a new look was in fact a disguised vacuum cleaner painted orange.

Changes in the script and story line also necessitated changes to the design approach. The return vehicle used to send the Helium-3 cannisters back to Earth was originally a series of silos sunk into the floor of the base that Gerty would load up with cannisters through the use of its mechanical arm. When it was decided that the Sam 2 clone would use the He-3 return vehicle as his method of getting back to Earth and evading the 'rescue team' sent to terminate him, it had to be rethought to accommodate a human body. Rothery redefined the concept as more of a lift, from which Sam 2 could remove the He-3 containers to make room for himself and his kit. These kinds of practical changes and revisions affected the look of *Moon* throughout production, altering the pre-visualisation conceptual art under the strain of low-budget twenty-first-century British filmmaking.

The approach of Rothery in his use of replicable 'key shapes' meant that areas of the moon base could be built out with a few overall large set pieces while still providing for enough visual variety throughout the sets as a whole. Each individual area in alcoves off the main corridors or central space was clearly designated for individual purposes, from Sam Bell's sleeping quarters, to his 'greenhouse' area, to the more industrial area where the He-3 cannisters are prepared for their journey to Earth. Rothery drew upon such NASA projects as the 2006 'reference architecture' for a potential human-occupied moon base on the edge of the Shackleton crater. The plan involved concepts such as human habitation modules, solar power units, unpressurised rover vehicles (so necessitating the wearing of space suits by drivers), and in-situ resource utilisation. This work was further expanded in 2008 with NASA's 'Lunar Surface Systems Concepts' study which offered funding for research into such elements of a lunar base as habitation units, rovers, and power production and storage. As well as being influenced by the science-fiction cinema of the 1970s, Jones and Rothery were absorbing contemporary thought on just how a manned presence on the moon might be established in the twenty-first century.

Even within the overall off-white colour scheme of the base, Rothery was happy to experiment in his CG renderings of the concept design. At one stage, he emulated James Cameron's *Aliens* by having red-hued emergency lighting that could come into play at dramatic moments. Almost as soon as the image was complete, Rothery recognised the concept broke the conceptual 'cleanness' of the overall look of the Sarang base. The idea was quickly dropped, but the no-cost (other than time) exploration of it through CG pre-visualisation had served to reinforce that Jones and Rothery were right in their initial minimal colour concept of the moon base. Such modern digital tools are vital to the work of designers in the low budget film arena, taking the visualisation of concepts far beyond the hand-painted 'concept art' pioneered by designers like Ralph McQuarrie on the original *Star Wars* trilogy or Ron Cobb on the likes of *Alien* or *Total Recall* (1990).

Lighting was important to the ultimate look of the sets. While much of this was down to director of photography Gary Shaw (his first feature as cinematographer, after years working in motion control photography) shooting in the 'real' moon base sets at Shepperton, Jones and Rothery had done much of the work during their pre-visualisations design period to develop the sets and lighting. The CG 3D rendering of the moon base set was an ideal playground in which to test out various lighting options. One element carried over into the production, but which is very subtly rendered, is the concept of utilising a 'daytime' and a 'night time' lighting scheme for the base interiors. While Rothery admitted to not being sure how well either of these lighting choices or the overall fully planned geography of the base comes across to the viewer, they are nonetheless emblematic of the obsessive attention to detail necessary to create a cohesive and convincing vision of the future that draws audiences into the world and holds their suspension of disbelief for the duration of the movie.

The cramming of screens into various nooks around the moon base was another accommodation of the film's low budget nature. The original hope had been to feature many more, much larger screens throughout, some perhaps relaying views of the exterior of the lunar surface. It quickly became clear that this option was simply too expensive, both in terms of set building and in terms of supplying visuals for the screens (or, indeed, expensive exterior views realised through CG animation). Instead, the screens became compacted into smaller areas, suggesting that when Sam needed to work on something he would retreat to these out of the way corners to concentrate. Instead, the monitors were more affordable options built into holes cut in the set, including multiple cheap LCD photo frames, small 15- and 19-inch screens, and only two larger screens (one at 28" the other at 40"). These were augmented by 'fake' monitors realised by building light boxes into the set onto which acetate printouts of screen graphics could be printed. These would be non-changing screen images (unless the acetate graphics were swapped out) but they were adequate enough for background scenes. This helped break up the possible bland emptiness of much of the modular design and gave some distinctiveness to particular areas.

Sam Bell's personal space was given special attention. Waking each lunar morning to the tune 'The One and Only', Sam was shown to exist within a domestic space he'd made some attempt to personalise. His bathroom area, where he has sketched the smiley faces that indicate the time elapsed since he arrived also features a child's drawing of a house and garden (representing the concept of home or Earth), surrounded by snapshots of his baby daughter Eve, animals (a cow is visible), and family groups, offset with a pair of child hand prints, presumably those of Eve. Photos of Tess surround some of the consoles that Sam accesses to control the smooth running of the base. His sleeping alcove is similarly adorned with photos pinned to the walls that serve as reminders of the life and the people he believes he has left behind on Earth. A framed photo of Tess takes pride of place on his bedside shelf (it must be special, as it is given the protection of a frame, unlike the other images adorning the walls). Wall posters and a couple of books and magazines complete the 'domestic' picture around this private area. It serves as a retreat for Sam, not just a sleeping area. It is his attempt to assert some control over his environment and his memories.

The unusual worn armchair suggests a favourite item that has been shipped from Earth to help Sam acclimatise to his new environment (even if he abuses it in his frustration over the broken satellite, piercing the armrest with his model knife). His work areas feature many Post-It notes, reminders of things to do or system passwords. Gerty, too, is adorned with sticky message reminders of action to be taken or tasks to be addressed ('Service Rover 3 Boom'). The model town is another non-essential addition to Sam's environment, functioning both as non-lunar related 'busy work' to keep his mind occupied and as another connection to home with the model based upon his hometown of Fairfield. All this suggests a man keen to maintain his connections with the life he has left behind.

Something quietly ignored by the filmmakers was that gravity on the moon is just one sixth of that of Earth. Pre-CGI, filmmakers often struggled to depict gravity-free experiences, using wires or actors miming in a kind of cod-slow motion. It was never particularly convincing, and in the worst examples it could come across as comic. *Moon* doesn't magic up an artificial gravity system (as depicted on the starships of *Star Trek*) to explain why Sam moves around the Sarang base without regard to the realities of near-weightlessness conditions. 'Lunar Gravity was something that we had quite a few chats about,' admitted Rothery on his blog, 'but in the end we couldn't afford to do a comprehensive sixth-gravity take over the entire film, so we just left it and it went away. Nobody's ever mentioned this to me so far, which I guess is a good sign.'

In keeping with the 'realism' approach applied to the interiors of the Sarang moon base, Jones and his team thoroughly researched the vehicles Sam Bell might use during the course of his three-year term. They knew that several 'rovers' would be required – one for Sam 1 to crash, and one for Sam 2 to drive out to retrieve his predecessor – and they also knew they'd need to show the Helium-3 'harvesters' in action to establish the process of mining and extraction that Sam was supervising. In addition, exterior shots of the base would establish a wider sense of place, as would the surrounding towers that are suppressing the real-time signals to and from Earth. Finally, they would need to show the lift off of the return vehicle that Sam 2 would use to escape the moon.

Some consideration was given to doing all vehicles, as well as all the moon surface material, through computer graphics. Budgetary breakdowns were worked out with visual effects house Cinesite to cost various approaches, from full-CG vehicles and moon exteriors to a mix of partial-CG and partial-model work. Guided both by cost considerations and his desire to emulate those 1970s cerebral science-fiction films that had so inspired his conception of *Moon* in the first place, Jones was keen to explore creating the vast majority of the vehicles and moon surface sequences using old-fashioned model miniatures. The production was lucky in employing the services of an about-to-retire Bill Pearson whose miniature model shop was conveniently based at Shepperton.

Pearson's team had three months to provide not only all the vehicles and lunar surface shots, but also create the space helmets and suits that the various Sam Bells would require (on science-fiction films, elements of costume design can often fall under the special effects side when it comes to building practical elements). Some of the Pearson team had experience stretching back to James Camerons *Aliens* (1986), so Jones felt in safe hands. The majority of the models were built at 1:12 scale (for mid- to long-shots), with one larger 'action' rover built at 1:6 scale (for close-ups; this one was in scale to accommodate a space-helmeted Action Man figure to represent Rockwell's Sam).

The rovers (and harvesters) were carved from Foamex, strong versatile plastic sheeting that was easy to bend, shape, and cut and could have textures and details printed directly upon it. The model-makers would follow Rothery's digital models for the rovers and then add what they called 'gubbins', the surface detail that made the vehicles look like actual functioning machines rather than Gerry Anderson-style *Thunderbirds* models from the 1960s (many of the model-makers on *Moon* expressed great admiration for the work of Anderson's chief model-maker, Derek Meddings, who graduated to big screen blockbusters like the 1970s Bond movies and *Superman: The Movie*, 1978). Detailed work even extended to the interior of the model rover cab, which would not even be seen on screen but helped build up the verisimilitude across the whole vehicle. Some tricks from the 1960s were still employed: forgoing complex radio control, the rovers in *Moon* were propelled across the lunar surface pulled by fine tungsten wire. These would be removed digitally in post-production. Cinesite would also augment the model shots with discrete CG touches, adding debris, lens flare, and other artefacts that would give the lunar surface shots a feeling of realism.

Largely deployed as a background vehicle, the lunar harvester that develops a fault and so brings Sam out to his near-fatal crash plays a crucial role in kick-starting the narrative. The core idea of extracting Helium-3 as the main concern of Lunar Industries came from the Robert Zubrin book *Entering Space* (1999) that explored the feasibility of deploying industrial processes on the moon. Zubrin speculated that Helium-3 would be very useful in any kind of fusion-drive energy generating process and while rare on Earth, huge deposits could be found just below the surface upon the moon. Jones positioned the mining effort on the dark side of the moon so the surface 'scars' would not be visible from Earth, and so the reflective qualities of 'moon light' that might affect animals on Earth would not be altered by the industrial mining process.

The concept of the harvesters was an autonomous vehicle which could scrape up the lunar regolith (the surface layer of deposits) and put it through a built-in industrial process to extract the He-3 gasses. The harvesters were essentially envisaged as mobile factories. The harvested He-3 gasses would then be compressed into canisters and multiple cannisters packed into a return vehicle back at the moon base. While the harvesters tirelessly continued their relentless work, the project's human supervisor would ensure a steady supply of He-3 reached a power-hungry Earth. In the two decades since Zubrin first proposed such industrial exploitation of Earth's nearest neighbour, the progress of renewable energy like solar and wind have developed making moon mining less needed.

For concept artist Gavin Rothery, it was important that the harvesters looked realistic, like machines driven by technology capable of doing the job. He took a 'hypothetical engineering' approach to his designs, attempting to reflect in the shape and movement of the vehicles the kind of internal processes that the industrial extraction of He-3 might imply. Believing that such an approach resulted in more convincing vehicles, Rothery built in such ideas as a location for the engine, the way the suspension might operate, and the kind of fuel that might drive such a vehicle. Each of these considerations was fed into developing the basic shape of the harvesters. Rothery also paid heed to the human element, adding a cockpit on the assumption that the harvesters would at some point require human attention, so that logically meant building in human access and control.

Graphic modelling software, such as 3DS Max, allowed Rothery to not only design his vehicles but to rotate them and view them from all angles. Essentially mobile factories, the harvesters were the most industrial looking design element of *Moon*. Rothery worked out that a huge amount of lunar soil would have to be extracted and processed even to produce small amounts of He-3 and so developed his mobile mining factory accordingly, taking into account that the process would also produce left-over 'waste' lunar soil that would have to be ejected back onto the surface. The Helium-3 accumulated on the moon's surface over billions of years, but it would only take a simple pass of an industrial process to denude the soil of it. A contemporary cash value for a ton of He-3 was estimated to be about $4 billion (in energy equivalent barrels of oil), making it a valuable resource for Lunar Industries to extract. The harvesters were designed to be in constant motion, with human supervisors having to use a rover to interface with the mobile factory. As with the rovers, when it came to designing the elements that go to make up *Moon*, form followed function.

The week-long model shoot for *Moon* took place after Sam Rockwell wrapped the live action shoot. One of the first issues was to find a suitable material to represent the lunar surface, across which several of the 1:12 and 1:6 scale vehicles would realistically drive. A large rostrum table was constructed for the lunar surface, but it couldn't be covered in one of the more traditional materials – Fuller's Earth, used to create the tornado in *The Wizard of Oz* (1939) – as its use had been restricted due to its connection with the construction of terrorist bombs. The solution was to use simple cat litter which could be built up into crater edges and delivered the perfect kick-up of dust when the large-wheeled rovers ran across it. For each change of lunar location, the surface was reshaped and reused. 'We only had one soundstage and one set for the model miniatures,' recalled Jones. 'We'd shoot all our stuff with ... the lunar base landscape. [That] would be taken out, [and] [Rothery] and I would spend the next hours creating a new lunar geography. It was madness.'[7]

Model-building also came into play in the creation of Sam Bell's robotic assistant, Gerty. While in the fiction of *Moon*, Gerty is seen to move around the Sarang moon base via a series of rails in the ceiling, on set there was no such rail line – this was all achieved through the use of CG. Instead, Rockwell had a life-size physical model of Gerty to interact with. Prior to that, the team had a life-size 2D wooden cutout blowup of the Gerty plans that Rothery had made to use on set for blocking purposes and to establish eye lines. The first design for Gerty was dubbed 'pac man', as it was an ovoid shape with a lighting 'halo' above it. It was designed to run on ceiling rails and to move vertically up and down a retaining rod. This was abandoned for being too high-tech for the industrial environment that Lunar Industries would have created at Sarang base. Rothery fell back on the idea of making Gerty resemble a group of old-style PC towers bolted together, as if he had been constructed out of several different computer systems. Rothery experimented by dropping various 'boxy' shaped Gertys into his already prepared 3D-renders of the moon base interior space to see how they looked within the environment. This helped the design process, resulting in a larger, more dominant Gerty (the 'pac man' variant looked lost in the expansive white environment). 'He was supposed to look like a bunch of modules semi-forced together,' said Rothery on his online blog. 'Also, it's much cheaper to fabricate boxy shapes than it is to do lots of bespoke curved surfaces, so we got another win there. Pretty much every decision we made during the making of this film was at least half-centered around saving some money.'

The final mix for Gerty between a physical model and a CG-assisted creation was about 60:40 according to Rothery. When first built, Gerty was supported on a large stand (removed in post-production) or mounted on a wheeled system, so he could move (also removed digitally). The ceiling rail system was hardly ever in shot, as this implied spending money on CG that the production couldn't afford; its existence was suggested by having Gerty's connection to the rail stretching upward out-of-frame. The finished Gerty model was a very clean, newly created object that had to be distressed to look like a well-used (having been in operation for at least 15 years) piece of equipment. An imaginative approach was adopted to 'dirtying down' Gerty involving coffee granules, stray graphic stickers, and purposely designed graphic elements. The result, according to Rothery, is that a coffee aroma followed Gerty around wherever he went. Old Post-It notes added to the 'used' effect. A small screen was built-in to accommodate the 'smiley face' emoji that would give Gerty so much personality. Four people were required to 'operate' Gerty when it was in action.

Gerty also had two separate articulated 'arms', built around a heavy custom-built metal frame, giving the robot the opportunity to manipulate its own environment.

These full-size arms were mounted on a base and pole which were initially painted blue for digital removal during post-production (when the cost of this became apparent, Rothery re-painted the support pole white and it effectively disappeared into the white-walled background); whereas in the fiction Gerty's main unit and the two arms were supported from the ceiling of the moon base, in actuality they were supported from the floor of the studio.

Kevin Spacey's voice-over for Gerty was completed in a single morning during post-production. During the shoot Jones had read in Gerty's lines, and both he and Rothery had got used to Gerty sounding uncannily like the film's director. It was clear that another voice would be needed, and Jones' connection with Spacey through his advertising work helped secure his contribution. As his voice-over was recorded so late in the process, Jones had a near-finished version of the film to show Spacey which helped seal the deal. Spacey ran through all of Gerty's lines twice during the recording session, leaving Jones to pick the best takes to use in the finished film.

The process of bringing Gerty to 'life' was yet another case on *Moon* where cheap-and-cheerful solutions were used to achieve a convincing high-tech look on camera. Sometimes, as the crew of *Moon* repeatedly demonstrated, the oldest, most easily achieved tricks of the movie trade beat out any amount of new-fangled CGI work, and they saved an awful lot of money too.

Moon's costume designer Jane Petrie had little experience of science-fiction or fantasy costume requirements, her only relevant credits being as a wardrobe assistant on 1999's *Star Wars: Episode I – The Phantom Menace* and as an assistant costume designer on 2004's live action *Thunderbirds*. Otherwise, she was much more at home on period pieces like *Gosford Park* (2001), *Vera Drake* (2004), and *Elizabeth: The Golden Age* (2007). Directed by Jones to immerse herself in 1970s and 1980s science fiction – as well as those films already mentioned, they included *Solaris* (1972) and *Outland* (1981) – and to design with an eye more on science fact than science fiction. With the period defined only loosely as 'the not too distant future', Petrie was able to ground much of her costume design work in the casual and industrial wear of today.

For Sam's frequently worn workwear, a combination maintenance overall and flight suit, Petrie directly referenced the look of Freeman Lowell (Bruce Dern) in *Silent*

Running. Both suits are covered in mission patches and commercial insignia, placing both characters clearly in the blue collar 'working class in space' zone. The majority of Sam's other outfits are more casual, with his floral Hawaiian shirt suggesting a call-out to that worn by Harry Dean Stanton's Brett in *Alien*. Both characters wear rather worn looking baseball caps. The spacesuit Sam wears when leaving the base to travel further afield in the rovers is a functional model echoing a streamlined version of the real-life NASA spacesuits, also used to good effect when Ripley (Sigourney Weaver) dons one in *Alien*.

Costuming was used to get to the heart of character and to differentiate between the two clones. As the film's original Sam 1 begins to deteriorate so his dress sense becomes ever-more sloppy and his clothes dirtier. As he declines further his clothes map that decline, with Petrie clothing the older Sam 1 in a slightly bigger and baggier version of the flight suit attire to almost suggest the degenerating clone was shrinking or losing body mass. In contrast, the trimmer and fitter newly born Sam 2 wears his tight-fitting flight suit fully zipped up, emphasising his more functional, straight edge approach to his new life. His clothes are cleaner and sharper edged, as they are new (just like him, and equally artificial). The costuming choices help the viewer make a clear distinction between the two Sams and their respective physical and mental development.

The most distinctive item of clothing was Sam Rockwell's own personal 'Wake me when its quitting time' T-shirt. Initially seen in the opening sequences as Sam exercises on a treadmill and gears up for his final few days on the moon base, it signifies his anticipation of his voyage home and his reunion with his wife Tess and daughter Eve. 'Quitting time', after three years, is finally within reach, only two weeks away. When the stored clones are discovered in the hidden drawers beneath the base, it is revealed that each clone is awakened with their own version of this T-shirt. The phrase 'Quitting time' can now be read in the light of the revelation that each of the previous Sam clones has been incinerated upon completion of the three-year contract: quitting in this sense is forever. These costume choices that echo character and plot are also reflected in the choice of Sam's 'wake up' song: Chesney Hawkes' 'The One and Only'. It appears innocuous enough at the beginning, but takes on a far more sinister connotation when Sam's clone status is revealed. Whatever

Sam Bell is, he is certainly not 'the one and only', just one of many.

The typography and graphic design of *Moon* is a fascinating area to look at in some detail. Drawing heavily on the work of Ron Cobb and the future-facing commercial graphic design of *Blade Runner*, Jones and Rothery set out to give *Moon* a real-world feel in its iconography. Rothery would end up producing at least 300 graphic elements, many of which he pasted to the walls of the Sarang moon base set, with the support of sign writer Julian Walker, in the final three days before shooting began. While they break-up the visual monotony of the all-white interior, the majority of the textual graphic elements are largely unreadable, even on Blu-ray. 'I was just making it all up as I went along as I could pretty much do what I wanted with the aesthetics of the base,' confessed Rothery on his blog. 'You can tell how short we were on manpower and time as there wasn't even time to proof read anything.' That resulted in some typographical errors, such as one sign referring to 'Heluim-3', which Rothery attempted to explain away as a deliberate misspelling by Lunar Industries so they could copyright the material they were producing! The food module boxes from which Sam Bell eats feature graphics depicting their contents – chicken, fish, fruit, beef – with accompanying graphic image. One, simply labelled 'Soylent' and featuring a stick-figure human image, is a shout out to one of Jones' filmic inspirations, 1973's *Soylent Green*. Rothery also designed the mission patches for Sam's flight suit, while a map created to work out the internal geography of the moon base was repurposed as an in-film graphic for a 'fire control' warning panel.

One of the most significant pieces of graphic design was that for the ever-present Lunar Industries logo. The final logo was made up of three elements, creating an L shape and two boxes contained within the L-frame, helpful reflecting the triple Helium-3 element at the centre of Lunar Industries' activities. Rothery had to work through what he termed many 'bad designs' before arriving at the one ultimately used on-screen. Drawing on corporate graphics from the 1970s he first came up with something 'jet age' and streamlined in origin, before opting for a circular 'moon'-type graphic orb and splitting the type horizontally, implying 'speed', for that all-important 'futuristic' look. As his designs got busier, he realised that a much-simplified logo would 'read' better on-screen.

He settled upon prioritising the word 'Lunar', that runs in large type above the subordinate 'Industries Ltd' which is in white text reversed out from a black bar that effectively underlines 'Lunar'. The chunky black 'L' with the two inset orange squares (meant to signify the 'I' of 'Industries') is also used on its own away from the full text. The font used was a sans serif Green Mountain 3 Microstyle. The black and orange colour was used throughout for other Lunar Industries safety notices and warning labels. The same font, logo, and colour scheme were worked into the Lunar Industries information film that opens the movie. There is a unity of theme and purpose in the final design that suits the elegance of the overall production of *Moon*.

Throughout where signage refers to the 'Sarang' base, it is accompanied by a Korean ideogram. The base was originally called 'Selene', reflecting its location on the moon, but Jones changed it late on to 'Sarang', the Korean word for 'love'. This was because he was in a long-distance relationship with a Korean woman at the time of *Moon*'s production. It fits the themes of the film, though, as Sam Bell is separated from those he loves, wife Tess and daughter Eve, but not only by the three years he imagines. In fact, as the 'real' Sam Bell is still on Earth and has lived the past 15 years with both Tess (until her death) and Eve: the Sams on the moon base are experiencing an out-of-date love.

For exteriors of the moon's surface and shots of both the moon and the Earth from space, Rothery employed digital matte paintings (DMPs) to give the low-budget production a grander scale. Unlike the film's other graphics, such as the typographic elements built into the Sarang moon base set, the DMPs were animated or featured camera movement to give them a sense of organic life or a feeling of travel and movement. They were – like much on *Moon* – simply achieved. Drawing upon reference images from books (Michael Light's *Full Moon*, 1999, was much consulted) and the internet, Rothery was able to bring life to otherwise still images.

The biggest challenge was the grey expanse of the lunar surface. It was important to build in some differentiation between various landscape features in order to offer a sense of contrast and to make the near-monochromatic images easier on the eye. The filmmakers used a commercially available 14-inch moon globe light (designed by Buzz Aldrin, the second man to walk on the moon in 1969) to gain a sense of the topography. Using a black marker pen, Jones picked out the exact places on the surface where the action would take place. Rothery would use areas of light and dark to help define the craters and mini mountains, using shade to disguise areas that were not of direct interest to the filmmakers. Placed next to more defined features, large dark areas would be read by the eye as simply another area of the landscape rather than the negative space it actually was.

Shots with either a partial moon or large Earth in the foreground while the Earth or the moon was seen as a whole sphere in the background were much featured, offering a solid sense of place and a relationship between the two celestial bodies mirroring that between the two Sam Bells. Combining elements of minimal movements, limited animation, and ambitious lighting schemes helped imbue these images with the sense of scale and place that Rothery was after. He would work up near-final roughs, animate them using commercially available computer-graphics packages, and then pass the material over to visual-effects house Cinesite for their guidance in creating the final images. These images were used as 'spacer' between scenes and particular sections of the film, giving a sense of pacing and of time passing as well as reminding audiences of the isolation of Sam Rockwell's character(s). A shot Rothery conceived, of a huge half-sphere partial moon looming above the tiny Earth was used under the opening titles, giving the Earth's natural satellite an ominous presence.

Most often, when an overhead shot of the moon's cratered surface was required, Rothery would devise an image featuring the 'terminator' where the sun's light shades off into darkness. This not only created a nice contrasting image, in which half was a photorealistic representation of the moon's surface and half was in mysterious darkness, but it also played into the themes. There is a dark secret at the heart of *Moon*: the hidden activities of Lunar Industries. The two-tone moon surface also echoes the twin Sam Bells. When Sam 2 appears, he is a lighter 'new born' presence in contrast to the darker moon-weary Sam 1 who wants to end his tenure and get back home to Earth.

The digital matte paintings were an economic solution to establishing time and place. They helped open out the film, as cost prohibited any views out onto the lunar surface from within the moon base. These kinds of shots had to be carefully chosen, as maintaining such computer-graphic heavy imagery in the background of a live action scene would have been very costly (Rothery put the cost at £8,000 to £12,000 per background shot). Fortuitously, Rothery was able to justify the closed-in nature of the Sarang base as also playing into the film's themes. 'We reconciled it as it contributing to Sam's sense of isolation and being closed off from the outside world,'[8] he wrote on his blog.

The design effort that went in to creating 'the look of the future' for *Moon* was all in service of the themes of the film. The sets and set dressing were optimised to play up to Sam Bell's initial sense of isolation and loneliness, while the huge lunar expanses depicted in the practical model work (enhanced by CGI) helped to solidify this sense of isolation. Costuming and the interior décor of the Sarang base also played to Sam's deteriorating mental and physical states. All this was achieved on an extremely limited budget and under strict time limitations. One of the key aspects of the distinctive look is how the democratisation of digital filmmaking tools such as CG pre-vis packages has helped make the pre-production process faster and more affordable. A $5 million movie like *Moon* could in 2008 access the kind of technology and production processes that would previously have been the arena of mega-budgeted Hollywood blockbusters. Such tools, however, could not replace simple creativity which remained constrained in the low-budget British feature film arena by lack of funds and facilities. The filmmakers involved in the creation of *Moon* achieved the near impossible on a budget and timescale that makes Sam Bell's three-year tenure look like an eternity.

Notes

1. Nicholas Pegg, *The Complete David Bowie* 6th ed. (London: Titan Books, 2011).
2. Angus MacKinnon, 'The Future Isn't What It Used to Be', *NME* (13 September 1980).
3. Gavin Rothery, 'Designing Sarang: Robotic Space-House of the Future', gavinrothery.com (21 August 2011) http://www.gavinrothery.com/they-never-went-to-the-moon.
4. Jeremy Owen, 'Gavin Rothery talks Moon (2009)', filminutiae.com (no date) http://filminutiae.com/take-07-moon-2009-gavin-rothery-interview.
5. Ibid.

6. Jeremy Owen, 'Gavin Rothery talks Moon'.
7. Simon Ward, *Making Moon: A British Sci-Fi Cult Classic* (London: Titan Books, 2019).
8. http://www.gavinrothery.com/they-never-went-to-the-moon?offset=1313923328000&reversePaginate=true.

Chapter Four: The Theology of *Moon*

In terms of production, Duncan Jones' *Moon* (2009) may have been a modest effort, but it packed a lot of ideas into its screenplay. As well as the issues of personal identity and what it is to be human (raised in Chapter Two), there is a theological undercurrent to much of the predicament of the various Sam Bells. Questions of purpose and the nature of the creator are immediately implicit in the revelation that the Sam Bell the viewer has been following early on is in fact simply one of an innumerable number of clones. Are the subsequent Sams any more or less 'real' than the first one encountered by the viewer, given that this 'original' Sam is in fact no such thing?

The first words uttered by Sam Bell on screen concern the four automated Helium-3 harvesters that he supervises. They are named Matt (for Matthew), Mark, Luke, and John – apparently names given to the harvesters by Sam himself, as they are written in crude marker pen above the displays indicating their operational status. The instigating incident is a fault that develops with the harvester designated Mark. 'We've got a live one on Mark,' Sam tells Gerty, his robotic companion. 'I'm going out to rope her in.' This leads to the accident that sees the next Sam Bell clone awakened – it is this clone that later discovers that Sam 1 who went to investigate Mark is still alive. The fourth harvester, which has been inoperable for much of Sam's three-year term of duty, was called Luke, but this has been furiously crossed-out to be replaced by the more judgemental moniker 'Judas'.

In the Bible and wider Christian tradition, Matthew, Mark, Luke, and John are deemed to be the authors of the four gospels of the New Testament named after them. Collectively, they are known as 'the four evangelists' whose writings are said to proclaim the 'good news' (or gospel) of Jesus, as suggested by Mark 1:1. Luke's redesignation as 'Judas' suggests that the failure of the fourth harvester is regarded by Sam as a betrayal of sorts, presumably because it has made it more difficult for him to achieve the desired targets for Helium-3 mining across his three years of service. Judas Iscariot is, of course, another key Biblical figure, the disciple who betrays Jesus in the Garden of Gethsemane. Little is made of the use of these names: they are rarely referred to by their names beyond this opening sequence and at a post-screening Q&A at the Sundance Film Festival screenwriter Nathan Parker denied they had any real significance. However, the unusual naming of the four harvesters and the replacement of Luke with Judas are clues to the theology of *Moon*.

There also appear to be Biblical meanings encoded in the very names of the key characters featured in *Moon*, suggesting that these names were not chosen by Parker and Jones at random or by accident. There is intelligent design evident in their selections. The central character (whatever variation of clone he may be) is named Sam, for Samuel (or the Biblical 'Shemu'el' of Hebrew origin), recalling the prophet of Israel featured in the Old Testament. Yet again, like the names given to the He-3 harvesters, Samuel is a key Biblical figure, venerated by Jews, Christians, and Muslims alike as a prophet. The Biblical Samuel played a significant role in the transition from the period of the judges to the kingdom of Saul and again in the move from Saul to David. The name Sam is understood to mean 'heard by God': in the Bible Samuel's mother Hannah prays to God for a child, a prayer heard and answered. According to Samuel 1:20, '[She] called his name Samuel, saying because I have asked him of the Lord'. Later, Samuel himself hears the voice of the Lord calling him, establishing him as a 'prophet of the Lord' and as a key player in the maintenance of the Israelite heritage and identity during the occupation by the Philistines. Samuel led the Israelites against the Philistines and gained a role as kingmaker in appointing Saul. In his combination of roles as prophet, priest, and ruler, Samuel is seen by Biblical scholars as a foreshadowing of the figure of Christ. While there appears to be no Biblical significance in Sam's surname of Bell, it is possible that it alludes to a scientific theory concerning Sam's helper, Gerty. The surname 'Bell' may have come from James Bell, creator of the concept of 'the technological singularity', when artificial intelligence surpasses human intelligence. If Sam Bell is 'heard by God', who or what is God in this construction: Gerty? Lunar Industries? Sam 2? Or someone else entirely? Perhaps it relates to the people of Earth who finally 'hear' of Sam's existence ...

Sam's daughter is named Eve, an obvious Biblical allusion. In the Book of Genesis, Eve is the first woman created by God. The name Eve generally means 'to breathe' or 'to give life' and has its roots in the Hebrew 'chavah' or 'havah'. The Eve the audience eventually meets is a teenager, while each iteration of the Sam Bell clones believes his daughter to be around three-years of age. Either way, she has not reached the 'giving life' stage of maturity.

Most intriguingly, there is Sam's wife, Tess. The name Tess, short for Theresa, or Esther, is of Greek origin and means 'harvester' or 'to harvest or reap'. The Biblical harvest meant survival, where the crops grown to maturity and reaped from the land would provide for the population through the barren winter months. The meaning of 'harvester' is especially relevant in the light of Sam's responsibility for the Helium-3 harvesters. It makes the choice of term 'harvester' rather than 'miners' for these automated tools even more interesting. The meaning of Tess also suggests some other concepts – she is the mother of Eve, and 'harvesting' can mean to 'bring to fruition' as in playing the role of a mother in raising or nurturing a child to maturity. The alternative meaning of 'to reap' recalls the phrase 'reap what you sow', meaning to suffer the just deserts of your actions. Perhaps this could point to the fate awaiting Lunar Industries when Sam 2 returns to Earth and goes public about their operations on the moon? This would also relate to his being 'heard'.

There are more names in *Moon* that can be similarly deconstructed, even if not all the meanings are of Biblical or religious origin. Sam's robotic assistant is named Gerty, a female name (diminutive of Gertrude) for a device given a male voice (Kevin Spacey). The meaning of 'Gerty' is 'strength of a spear' or 'strong spear' and is of Germanic origin. It was a popular name in the second half of the nineteenth century, but its usage rapidly declined in the United States from the 1940s onwards. Gerty's 'strength' might be interpreted in the robot's final decision to help Sam, following its primary programming to be of assistance to him and keep him safe. When Gerty initially appears and is heard to speak in calm measured tones that echo those of Douglas Rain in his voicing of HAL-9000 in *2001: A Space Odyssey* (1968), it is easy for the audience to assume that Gerty will ultimately turn out to be a malevolent obstacle that Sam will have to overcome. That turns out not to be the case, and while Gerty is fully aware of Lunar Industries use of multiple Sam Bell clones, it doesn't appear to see a role for itself in necessarily covering up these actions. Once the two Sam Bells are active, Gerty appears to do its best to aid both of them, ultimately playing a significant role in Sam's escape to Earth at the climax.

Finally on the naming front, there is the 'rescue' ship sent to retrieve Sam by Lunar

Industries – while this is described by the company as a rescue mission, both Sam and the audience interpret the dispatch of the ship as a threat, a possible 'clean up' mission aimed at eliminating Sam and hiding the company's complicity in the cloning conspiracy. The ship is named *Eliza*, another Biblical reference being the name of the mother of John the Baptist in the Old Testament. Eliza means 'oath of God', suggesting that the company has an 'oath' to protect itself and its investments, and in terms of Sarang base, may even view itself as 'God', master of all it has created, including the Sam clones. The company may also be honouring an 'oath' to provide Earth with cheap and clean energy.

There is a clash embedded at the heart of *Moon* between these Biblical or religious notions sourced in the naming of the characters and the depiction of a scientifically-driven universe where technology is given primacy over humanity – Sam Bell himself, as a clone, is simply another technological product ultimately owned by Lunar Industries, created to do a simple job and, therefore, disposable. Science is given primacy, both visually and in the text of *Moon*. It is science that has put man on the moon and allowed for the harvesting of Helium-3 to provide cheap energy back on Earth. None of this is a matter of religious faith, but do the secrets hidden in the character names suggest an alternative reading?

Could the original Sam Bell, the source template for the clones, have been a religious man? There is little to suggest this from what we see of Sam and Tess' home on Earth or of their daughter, Eve. Sam has a handful of possessions on the moon, among them a several books, but none of these appears to be a Bible. If he'd wanted to, Jones could easily have suggested such a subtext with a simple shot of a Bible on Sam's bookshelf. However, there is the naming of the harvesters after books of the Bible, an individual act carried out (in marker pen) by Sam, not an official designation by Lunar Industries. Where does the motivation for Sam to adopt this naming protocol come from, and where does the urge to rename Luke as 'Judas' originate? The harvesters could just as easily have been named after the members of the Beatles (John, Paul, George, and Ringo) or the Teenage Mutant Ninja Turtles (Leonardo, Raphael, Michelangelo, and Donatello) if Jones were looking for a quartet of names to make a pop culture reference. The use of these Biblical names suggests an obscured deeper meaning.

Could Sam Bell himself be regarded as a form of God? He is the sole human alive on the moon (at least initially) and is in charge of all he surveys. Further, he is engaged in an act of creation (or re-creation) in his obsessive building of a model town patterned after his home town of Fairfield, where his family – Tess and Eve – live (perhaps a new Jerusalem). The second revived Sam Bell clone, in rebelling against the instruction from Gerty that he should not leave the moon base recalls the actions of Adam and Eve in the Garden of Eden, rebelling against the word of God and sampling the knowledge implied in the eating of the apple, or of the rebellion of the fallen angel Lucifer. The Latin 'Lucifer' means Light-Bringer, which positions Sam Bell as both a Jesus figure, born to sacrifice himself for the (Capitalistic) sins of the world, and Lucifer, bringing literal light (in the form of Helium-3 derived energy) to the world.

Sam, too, gains forbidden knowledge when he discovers his injured predecessor out on the moon's surface which leads to his decoding of his own nature as a clone. His rebellion and acquisition of this knowledge reveals secrets that Lunar Industries (perhaps the true 'God' in this scenario) would rather keep occulted. Ultimately, the technology and science of the world of *Moon* overrides any meaning hidden in the naming of the characters, just as technology and science replaces religious faith in enlightened societies. Technology both allowed for the creation of the Sam Bell clones and, ultimately, allows for one of them to escape the 'garden' of the moon and return to Earth to reveal the secret at the heart of Lunar Industries exploitation of the planet's only natural satellite. There is another possibility: Sam Bell is engaged in a life of service, followed by sacrifice, salvation, and redemption after three years. Perhaps Sam is not an analogy for God but for Jesus Christ.

There is yet another, fundamental Biblical tale echoed in *Moon* – that of the resurrection. The Anastasia of Christ can be found in the plight of *Moon*'s various incarnations of Sam Bell. As each clone is awakened, Sam is effectively raised from the dead through his replacement with a new, fresher model. At the end of each three-year contract period, the clone itself appears to be in state of decay, as seen through the gradual physical deterioration of the first Sam. Persuaded to enter the pod that is supposed to return him to Earth, the previous Sams have each been incinerated, suffering a genuine death. There is no need for Gerty to wait the Biblical three days before unpacking the next Sam in line. In fact, the robotic assistant's eagerness to move on to the new model Sam 2 without confirming the death of the missing Sam 1 leads to the revelation of their nature as clones. Sam's repeated deaths and 'resurrections' would be followed-up by Jones in his next movie, *Source Code* (2011), in which Jake Gyllenhaal's operative Colter Stevens re-experiences the same events in an effort to track down a terrorist bomber, being 'killed' when he runs up against the eight-minute time limit within which he can exist and re-exist.

The revival and replacement of the various Sam Bell clones, re-enacting the Biblical concept of the resurrection of Jesus Christ, usually runs in a three-year cycle. The number three (we see a trio of Sam Bell clones: the two who are active and the one revealed in storage and activated at the end) recurs frequently in the Bible and in Christian theology where it is denoted to represent concepts of wholeness, completeness, or perfection. The Christian doctrine of the Trinity explores the three aspects of God: the Father, the Son (Jesus Christ), and the Holy Spirit. There are many examples of three as symbolic or meaningful in the Bible, from Noah's three sons (Genesis 6:10) to the three visitors who appear to Abraham (Genesis 18:2). With particular relevance to Sam Bell, there are the three days Christ was in his tomb following the Crucifixion prior to his resurrection (Luke 24:7). Jonah spent three days and nights trapped inside the whale (Jonah 1:17) just as each Sam Bell spends three years 'trapped' within the moon base. The Trinity and obsession with three (the number is used 467 times in the Bible[1]) is also reflected in the notion that human beings depend upon the trio of head, heart, and hands for a balance in life. Thinking, believing, and doing are at the core of everything that drives Sam Bell, especially when it comes to the inquiry into his own nature – it is this alone that brings him to 'completion' or 'wholeness', the power of three.

Several times Sam Bell is 'awakened', comes to consciousness, and understanding of himself and his place in the world, a view expanded by his discovery of his 'true' nature as the direct artificial creation of another. We only fully see this process once, as Sam 2 is brought to life by Gerty as a replacement for the model that has gone missing, but it is suggested that the process has taken place about five times in all over a span of 15 or so years.

With awakening comes self-knowledge. The situation the two Sams find themselves in has never happened before, and given how unrestrained Gerty is to enact the process of awakening another, there seem to be no technological nor bureaucratic obstacles to this happening. No verification of the 'death' of the previous Sam appears to be required (a basic safeguard Lunar Industries might have built-in to prevent exactly this scenario – the accidental awakening of a replacement Sam when the previous iteration has not been vaporised – from occurring). For many societies, the foundation of all spiritual growth and personal development is the awakening of self-awareness. For most of humanity, such self-awareness is actively avoided as it would imply action or a need to make a change. From the evidence seen in *Moon*, specifically references to Sam Bell having tamed his temper over three years, it seems the clones can engage in a process of self-development. Isolation and concentration on his work (whether with the harvesters or in the building of his model village) has allowed Sam to confront his own failings in this area.

Being alone, Sam is not subject to the criticism of others, until his other self turns up. Humans in social groups help enforce societal norms on each other. It is clear from the moment we first see Sam that he has let his physical appearance go: he has a straggly beard and looks generally unkempt (this also may be evidence of the deterioration in this clone's physical condition at the end of life).

Confronted by this self-knowledge (depicted through knowledge of another self), Sam gains an understanding of his own nature, but can this understanding be said to be of benefit to him? Perhaps each of the previous Sam Bell clones were happier in their ignorance, unaware of their precise nature, simply going through the motions of their job, living and dying in a brief three-year span, unaware they were simply the latest model in what was clearly intended to be a long line of disposable Sam Bells. Ultimately, while it may give him some troubles in the short term, this self-knowledge is beneficial to Sam. It allows Sam 2 to escape, while Sam 1 (along with Gerty) makes the sacrifice necessary to send him on his way. Sam 2's return to Earth reveals the Lunar Industries conspiracy and ultimately frees over 150 of his fellow clones.

Each new clone is awakened in the Sarang base medical centre, a plain white room, small and narrow, almost cave-like. While the Sams do not have to roll aside a rock blocking their way as Jesus did when emerging from the Holy Sepulchre, at 18 minutes into the movie the 'newly-born' Sam 2 does face a moment of confusion as he awakes clad in a Lunar Industries-branded 'shroud'. He has to ask where he is and cannot recall any accident (as this Sam did not experience an accident). Gerty indicates a requirement to keep Sam in the infirmary for a few days (perhaps three?) for a full recovery to take place. When Sam 2 does try to leave, he is weak and collapses. After returning to his quarters, but still not on active duty, Sam dreams of Tess. This is interrupted by his vision of another, spacesuit-clad Sam clawing his way up from beneath the sheets of his bed suggesting the return of either buried knowledge or of an earlier personality. There is purity in rebirth, a return to the native state, yet also corruption in knowledge, a change from the native state.

From the earliest of 'scientific romances' through to the era of blockbuster movies, science fiction has often concerned itself with the transcendent, matters of faith, and of religion. At the basis of much science fiction, whether literary, or on television or in movies, has been 'the outward urge' (as British author John Wyndham dubbed man's exploration of space), the desire to know what lies beyond Earth, to know who or what might be out there and to seek out new meaning from such encounters. The exploration of religion and faith underpinned much Western science fiction from the pulps of the 1920s to the 'new wave' of the 1960s. The alien as God-like was a regular feature of such tales, pitting human rationalism against perceived alien superiority (whether technological, sociological, or moral). Post-apocalyptic tales often depicted a world fallen to barbarism and superstition, sometimes shown to be religious in nature (as in Walter M. Miller Jr.'s 1960 novel *A Canticle for Leibowitz*). False Gods proliferate and false idols are worshipped (in the 1970 sequel *Beneath the Planet of the Apes*, the object of sacrilegious worship is an unexploded atomic bomb).[2]

There is a rich and deep tradition of exploring religion within literary science fiction. From the one-religion-per-planet trope in *Star Trek* (1966-1969) to the many religions of *Babylon 5* (1993–1998, see especially the episode 'Believers') television too has tackled the subject, however superficially. In movies, there is the mysterious all-powerful Force of the *Star Wars* saga (1977–present), to depictions of Superman as an alien God on Earth (*Man of Steel*, 2013), and the 'ancient aliens' of *Prometheus* (2012). That Ridley Scott movie (a belated prequel to his own *Alien*, 1979) raises many of the same questions that the plight of Sam Bell brings up in *Moon*: Who created us? Why are we here? What is our purpose? Rather than shy away from these issues, screenwriter Nathan Parker and director Duncan Jones have deeply embedded them in the text of *Moon*, making these issues central to the story they have to tell.

Each human being believes themselves to be unique. The use of the Chesney Hawkes song 'The One and Only' as Sam Bell's regular wake-up alarm may initially appear to be little more than a knowing joke indicative of Sam's self-perception, later cruelly undermined by the revelation of his status as just one of many Sam Bell clones, but a close consideration of the song's lyrics reveal just how apt it is to the overall thematic concerns of *Moon*, including its theology.

The opening verse of the song contains the telling lines: 'And yet you try to make me forget / Who I really am / Don't tell me I know best / I'm not the same as all the rest'. Each new Sam Bell clone is supposed to be unaware of its predecessors ('You try to make me forget / Who I really am'). Being a clone, every Sam is identical (at least to begin with) making the line 'I'm not the same as all the rest' as ironic as the song's title in this context. Hawkes says 'Call me, call me by my name or call me by number', but Sam Bell doesn't yet know he is simply the latest 'number' (in this case #5) in a long line of clones.

There are other lyrics that echo the plight of Sam in *Moon*, such as 'You put me through it' (perhaps alluding to Lunar Industries abuse of the clones); 'My soul embraces one more in a million faces' (another suggestion of Sam's true nature as one clone of many, knowledge somehow held in Sam's 'soul'); 'High hopes and aspirations, and years above my station' (Sam hopes to return home to Tess and Eve, after his years spent at his station); and 'I've tried to walk with dignity and pride' (suggesting Sam's ultimate nature as an empathetic human being). Other lyrics can be read as addressing Lunar Industries and Sam's plight as their pawn, such as 'I can't wear this uniform without some compromises' and 'For this job, I'm the best man'. Ultimately, the song concludes: 'I am the one and only / You can't take that away from me' addressing Sam's unique human nature.

Over the first 20 minutes or so, *Moon* turns from being an observational account of one man's (boring, routine) work to being an investigative narrative in which the subject of the investigation is ultimately himself. Sam Bell's daily routine for almost three years has been to tend to the harvesters. When problems arise, he deals with them – that's his primary function, it is why Lunar Industries have a live human on the moon rather than a more sophisticated version of Gerty. Presumably the thinking is that a human can be more imaginative in his reactions to the problems that arise and therefore better equipped to come up with innovative solutions, where a machine – no matter how sophisticated – can only react as far as its programming allows.

One of the aspects absent from computers like Gerty is curiosity. It is his human curiosity that will drive Sam Bell to ask questions, but not just any questions: the right questions. The relationship between questions, curiosity, and learning as inquiry is dubbed the Inquiry Cycle[3] in pedagogic practice. In this continuous enquiry, such questions 'are the root of inquiry; they initiate, sustain, and invigorate each aspect of the process. Questions direct investigations, drive creativity, stimulate discussion, and are the bedrock of reflection.' Being driven to question is not enough on its own; investigation requires a detailed confrontation with that being questioned, as Sam Bell discovers.

When Sam 2 is awakened, he quite quickly comes to suspect that something is not right. The story of the crash does not seem to add up, and he overhears Gerty seemingly having a real-time conversation with the Earth-bound representatives of Lunar Industries, despite Gerty's insistence that 'We've been having some problems with the lunar sat and our live feed seems to be down'. When Sam 2 realises he cannot leave the base and orders come from Earth for Gerty to prevent him from exiting, he knows something is definitely not right. He has questions, but no answers.

These unanswered questions provoke action – Sam engages in some light sabotage, faking a fault that requires him to go outside and persuading Gerty to let him attend to it. It is this desire for knowledge, to know what is going on, that brings Sam 2 out to the stalled harvester where he discovers Sam 1, still alive in the crashed rover. Returning to the Sarang base with Sam 1 in tow, Sam 2 cannot get any answers from

Gerty to his repeated pleas of 'Who is he?' The revived Sam 1, given sight of Sam 2 standing by the medical bed, is driven to ask the same question: 'Who is he?'

This question is at the centre of *Moon*: who is Sam Bell? The two Sams are allowed to co-exist as Gerty is simply following its core programming to protect Sam Bell, no matter how many of them there may be. Gerty doesn't appear to distinguish between the two Sams, treating them equally, judging that both have an equal right to exist: 'I'm here to keep you safe, Sam'. Within each Sam, however, there is a different process going on. Each Sam believes himself to be 'the one and only', so the shock appearance of a doppelgänger takes a while to come to terms with. Their initial interactions are of shock, amazement, and disbelief, soon followed by curiosity. It is this curiosity and the drive to ask the 'right' questions to elicit useful knowledge that drives Sam Bell's Inquiry Cycle. These questions provide a call to action: the situation demands a response.

The process of inquiry sees the two Sams slowly come to terms with each other's existence. 'You look just like me. It's incredible,' says Sam 1, only for Sam 2 to respond: 'Why do I look like you? Why don't you look like me?' Sam 1's conclusion – 'We look like each other, I guess' – can be seen as the point where the two Sams overcome their initial hostile reactions and begin to come to terms with the undeniable fact of their mutual existence. It's a moment of truce between the two humans, each attempting to claim primacy over the right to 'be' Sam Bell. From this point they work together to investigate the very fact of their unusual existence.

Concepts of knowledge and ignorance are central to religion. The big questions surrounding humanity are considered, if not answered, through such approaches as religion, sociology, and science. At a fundamental level, religion relies upon belief rather than empirical knowledge, while the scientific method requires such 'belief' to be tested through repeatable experimentation. As a human stationed on the moon to supervise a quartet of Helium-3 harvesters, Sam Bell is a product of this scientific approach. However, the questions that confront him when he begins to investigate the true nature of his existence belong firmly within the religious realm. Where faith and knowledge are often positioned as opposites, Sam Bell requires both to overcome his unusual predicament.

Throughout the past four or five clone iterations, Sam has been entirely ignorant of his true status. For each three-year cycle, he has believed himself to be a singular human, working out his time so he can return to his wife and daughter on Earth. A systemic conspiracy has been erected around him, consisting of the real-time communications black out, the seemingly wilful ignorance of Gerty, and a series of fake (and, through each iteration of Sam, presumably repeated) messages from Tess on Earth (which may have been sent to the original Sam Bell, assuming he actually served the first three-year term before being replaced by the clones – there is nothing within the text to clarify if this was the case, or if only clones have ever been present on the moon).

The philosophical science fiction of *Moon* questions the purpose of human existence, the central point of much religion. When asking to shake Sam 2's hand, Sam 1 is expressing his loneliness. He has been on his own (as far as he is aware) for three years, without any real-time human contact. Everything from Earth is mediated at a distance through not only a screen but through time, as the messages are all pre-recorded and cannot be directly interacted with. His only company has been Gerty, a robotic assistant whose primary role is to keep Sam 'safe', but not necessarily to aid in securing his mental health. It comes as little surprise, then, that Sam regularly talks to the handful of plants he cultivates (it is witnessing this devotion that provokes Sam 2 to ask Sam 1 how long he has been on the moon) and subsumes himself in the task of building his insanely detailed replica model of his home town. These are displacement activities, to keep him occupied and to prevent him from asking questions of himself: who is he and what is his purpose in life (questions that are often regarded as the preserve of religion)?

Despite his loneliness, Sam has not been driven to ask these questions until the arrival of Sam 2. He is a working-class drone, engaged in his task and oblivious to much that goes on around him. Despite having abundant time, he has not questioned his role, simply believing that when he has served out his three years, he will return home. This is an article of faith for each Sam clone that has been awakened: Lunar Industries has his best interests at heart (hence Gerty's concern for his safety) and will see him safely home at the end of his contract. In a way, when each deteriorating Sam clone is incinerated at the end of the three years, they are indeed returned 'home': dust-to-dust, ashes-to-ashes (for we know Major Tom's a junkie).

Work and reward are at the centre of Sam's existence. For a long time, these same concepts have been at the centre of the organisation of many Western societies, a system that is beginning to break down in the early twenty-first century thanks largely to the kind of increasing automation of which both Gerty and the harvesters serve as prime examples. As far as can be determined, the previous Sams have spent little to no time questioning the set-up of Lunar Industries of which he is a pivotal part. He doesn't question the economic implications of his own existence. He doesn't seem to have given much thought to the bigger picture. It is only when he gets together with himself (in the form of Sam 2) that some of these questions begin to occur to him. As they slowly come to the realisation that there must be yet more Sam Bells secreted somewhere on the base, the bigger picture comes into focus for Sam 2. 'It's a company, right?' he says of their employer, Lunar Industries. 'They have investors, they have shareholders, shit like that. What's cheaper, spending time and money training new personnel or you just have a couple of spares here to do the job? ... Do you really think they give a shit about us? They're laughing all the way to the bank!'

This concept is at the heart of *Moon*'s take on the world of work and reward. Lunar Industries have eliminated the 'reward' part of the deal, although they use the mirage of a reward (a return to Earth, to Tess and Eve), maintained through an elaborate and repeated deception, to keep each Sam Bell clone in line until each three-year period elapses. The Sam Bell clones are simply another asset for Lunar Industries, true 'human resources' but without the responsibility required with actual humans. Gerty's role of keeping Sam safe is not a replacement for proper employment laws and protections, it is more the function of a night watchman in keeping an eye on valuable property.

As in much science fiction, whether on screen or of the literary variety, this is simply an exaggeration of a reality in the world today. Lunar Industries is just the ultimate expression of the zero hours contracts, insecure employment, and low-regulation workplaces that make up much of the modern work environment. The search for ever greater efficiency in process, with the ultimate aim of increasing profit and shareholder value, is the driving force behind many companies. The larger the corporation, the more likely it is to treat its workforce as replaceable, disposable units of production. The Sam Bell clones are simply the ultimate example. The fact that the Lunar Industries programme on the moon is apparently being conducted in secret suggests that even at this future point such practices would still be widely regarded as simply unethical (and that's before you get into the questions surrounding the issue of human cloning).

Moon argues that dehumanisation and corporate greed go together, that the former may be an inevitable outcome of the latter. Such exposés through fiction have a long history. Upton Sinclair's *The Jungle* (1908) investigated the lives of immigrant workers in Chicago, exposing the harsh conditions and exploitation they faced working in the meat-packing industry. The companies treated their workers as expendable, completely replaceable thanks to an endless source of labour. Reforms followed Sinclair's work, but there have been many more Sinclairs and many more reforms in the near 120 years since, but nothing much has changed. The basic exploitation of labour continues to drive Western capitalism. The long-expected life of leisure promised by increasing industrialisation is yet to emerge. *Moon*'s cloned workforce is simply another example of corporate greed over-ruling any ethical concerns in the pursuit of profit with a nice side benefit for humanity (a source of cheap energy) offered in the way of cover. This kind of ethical off-setting is common to larger companies operating today who excuse their exploitation in the name of the greater good.

A combination of deception and self-deception has kept the Sam Bell clones productive, with each working through to the end of multiple three-year contracts until the film opens. The promise of reward (usually a pay packet that enables a certain lifestyle) is what keeps workers engaged in their jobs. For Sam, his return home is a matter of belief, but how is this belief matrix enforced?

Implanted memories and the control of information result in the manufacture of belief in Sam Bell. It is clear that at the point of awakening, each Sam is exactly alike not only in looks and personality but also in memories and 'experiences'. They all start from the same base level, having left his wife Tess and his young daughter

Eve behind on Earth to spend three years working on the moon for the big pay day that presumably would mean that Sam wouldn't ever have to work again. This is the point where the genuine Sam Bell departs from the experience of his clones – he did return to Earth and has continued with his life, Tess having died at some point, and Eve now a teenager. For the Sam clones on the moon, none of this has happened. They are maintained in a state of ignorance of the real world outside of the Sarang base by the machinations of Lunar Industries, held in a constant stasis, a repeating 'present' that the 'real' world on Earth has long left behind.

The awakened Sam 2 is fresher, younger, and more driven than the blasé, tired, and worn-out Sam 1 who, until the arrival of his clone, was simply looking forward to completing his contract and returning home. 'I'm going back. That's it for me. I've got a contract,' says Sam 1, when the news of the rescue vehicle reaches the moon. 'I'm going home.' It is Sam 2 who immediately realises the significance of the 'rescue' team – they are no such thing, being instead a clean-up squad to bury the secret of the clones. Sam 1 is so set in his ways that despite the evidence before his eyes in the shape of a 'newer' version of himself, he is still trapped within the orthodoxy of thinking that the company has implanted within him, all the better to control him. As the film's iconic poster declares: '250,000 miles from home, the hardest thing to face is … yourself.'

This self-deception and belief in the 'goodness' of the company are akin to the role of faith in religion. For Sam 1, his world was simple. He was engaged to do a job, albeit one that involved being away from home for a significant period. That high level of inconvenience meant a significant pay out at the end. Sam could not be sure of receiving his reward until the end of his residence on the moon, just as those who believe in their 'reward' in the afterlife have to simply take it on faith that they will actually get to enjoy it. It is only Sam's questioning of himself, his self-examination (through the gimmick of an identical clone) that awakens him to the reality of his plight. Confronted by what his other self uncovers (the secret stash of yet more Sam Bell clones), Sam is forced to abandon mere faith and to confront the hidden truth of his existence. He has been deliberately maintained in ignorance of reality to benefit Lunar Industries (they might also argue that such enforced ignorance was also for his own benefit, as a limited life-span clone). Sam 1 realises that he never actually met the real Tess or Eve, that they are simply implanted memories. Tess and Eve as concepts have kept the Sams going, believing in the scenario of a return to Earth and life with his family, giving him something to strive for, a reward to be gained through suffering. His new self-knowledge destroys that faith, removing simple belief. Lunar Industries' construct collapses.

It is confronting himself that breaks Sam Bell out of his Lunar Industries-induced stupor. He has spent the previous three years on the moon without any other in-person human connection. Arguably, he has retreated into himself, into an interior world, as a method of survival, a way of simply seeing through his three-year term by minimising himself. The arrival of Sam 2 destroys the belief that has been manufactured for him by Lunar Industries. Ironically, it is another Lunar Industries creation, Sam Bell clone #6, that is instrumental in this mental awakening.

Sam 1's empathy for another human being (ironically, a younger iteration of himself) is brought to the surface only when he has to interact with Sam 2. It has been slowly eroded across the three years of his existence, perhaps as much as a method of self-protection as anything else. Once the two Sams get past their mutual incredulity and continued self-belief that they are 'the one and only', the pair bond over their shared plight. Sam 2 is sharper, as he's fresher out of the box, than Sam 1. He hasn't suffered the same period of loneliness as Sam 1, whose faculties, mental as well as physical, seem in terminal decline by this point in his life cycle. After a bout of ping-pong, the two Sams bond over their shared memories of Tess and Eve, as well as their physical fight over the model table. Both of these elements of their lives are, of course, as fake as they are, fake people with false memories. Does this bonding over imaginary memories make them less human, less individual? If they cannot escape their 'programming', can they ever be truly human?

It has often been said that a man is the sum of his memories – it's a quote that has turned up across popular entertainment, from *Assassin's Creed* to *Doctor Who*. This theory of 'holism', that the individual parts of the whole are in intimate interconnection, so much so that they cannot exist independently, can be successfully applied to the Sam Bell clones. On their own, each of them has been less than fully human. They have not enjoyed human interaction or human society (despite their false memories convincing them that they have). Together they are better able to simulate something closer to humanity. In their argument, disagreement, and ultimate resolve to action, they join together to form a whole human being. This externalises the kind of self-reflection that normally takes place within a single individual, with pain suffered being a spur to change.

Caritas is defined as 'Christian love of human kind' and it was central to *Blade Runner* (1982) creator Philip K. Dick's definition of the authentically human. It was the ability to develop empathy (the ability to share and understand the feelings of another person) and to display *caritas* that marked out the true human in contrast to the android, replicant, or clone. The clones in *Moon* are designed to fulfil a task, and they are gifted with the minimal humanity required to achieve that. It is only when the two clones are brought together that they, combined, are able to develop a degree of self-awareness that was previously missing. In the case of the Sam Bells, it is empathy and *caritas* for another version of himself, but the process results in more rounded human action, where questions are raised, and the answers result in decisive action that fundamentally changes things.

The Bible tale of the scapegoat (Leviticus 16:20–21) is also relevant to Sam Bell's plight in *Moon*. He and his fellow clones have been put in the position of the scapegoat, in this case made to suffer for the benefit of others. He is born, works, and dies alone, across a short period of time, over and over again, so that many millions on Earth can benefit from economical energy. Philosopher William James adopted this very definition in an address to the Yale Philosophical Club in 1891, describing a world in which 'millions [are] kept permanently happy on the one simple condition that a certain lost soul on the far-off edge of things should lead a life of lonely torture.' James asked what kind of society it would be that could 'deliberately accept the fruit of such a bargain'.[4]

In *Moon*, Sam Bell and his fellow clones are William James' 'lost soul' condemned to 'a life of lonely torture' in order that 'millions [are] kept permanently happy'. Is some form of sacrifice necessary to benefit those on Earth making use of the cheap energy that harvesting the moon's Helium-3 brings them? Are they aware and do they care? Do the benefits outweigh any concern about the reality of such exploitation? This is a reality in our world today, in the exploitation of impoverished workers in far-off countries in the creation of cheap clothes for high street stores – do the purchasers of the finished affordable items give any thought to how they are created? Is an annual charity donation (another meaning of *caritas*) enough to off-set the moral qualms involved?

This combination of what might be thought of as the scapegoat bargain with the moral dimension of the plight of James' 'certain lost soul' defines the limited life(s) of Sam Bell. It is his fate to be sacrificed repeatedly in order to benefit a far greater extent of humanity, and it is his curse to be unaware of the true nature of his sacrifice. As far as he knows, he's working out a limited-period contract, then returning home. He's unaware of his eventual destruction, even as it happens, as it is disguised as the process by which he might be blasted back to Earth in a space capsule. The next clone arrives fresh into the world of Sarang base, ready to re-enact the entire ritual over again. This foundational moral dilemma has been explored by a variety of authors, from Fyodor Dostoyevsky's *The Brothers Karamazov* to Ursula K. Le Guin's short story *The Ones Who Walk Away From Omelas*. As writer Henry Little put it: 'The benefit of "society" wreaks substantial, lethal and ontologically disruptive physical changes upon the individual subject.'[5]

Humanity's moral perfection is not the concern of Lunar Industries. Industry and the profit from it are all that they are focused on, so the 'suffering' of a handful of human clones hardly factor in their calculations of the bottom line, their profit. The 'far of edge of things' is the far side of the moon, where alone and largely forgotten the harvesters and Sam Bell toil, unacknowledged and ultimately unrewarded with anything but death. It is doubtful that the general population of Earth is aware of the details of their cheap energy source – its existence and availability are enough. The complications of how it happens are simply not of interest to consumers, as with today's 'fast fashion'. According to the brief cameo scene in Jones' *Mute* (2018), it is Sam 2's successful return to Earth that exposes the Lunar Industries conspiracy. Prior to this event, it appears to have been a case of 'out of sight, out of mind' for most of Earth's population.

In *Moon*, Parker and Jones successfully dramatise the ancient moral questions of the scapegoat bargain. They built on the work of James, Dostoyevsky, Le Guin, and many others to depict this moral dilemma in the form of an accessible popular entertainment. *Moon* is a character-driven thriller that establishes a norm, then destroys it, resulting in change. Like those thoughtful science-fiction movies of the 1970s – *Silent Running* (1972), *Soylent Green* (1973), *Logan's Run* (1976) – *Moon* engages with contemporary questions and gives them an enduring moral spin. It encodes within its human drama (if that term can be applied to a pair of clones) a series of abstract, philosophical questions that can be engaged with by the committed viewer while not getting in the way of the enjoyment of the more casual movie fan in a way that, say, both versions of *Solaris* (1972, 2002) failed to. The unanswered question of *Moon* is how wider humanity deals with this scapegoat question when it is unavoidably brought to its attention.

Despite all the religious allusions and the game-playing with character names, *Moon* can ultimately be read as an atheist allegory that highlights the inhumanity of much organised religion and opts for a view of the world that has no place for God, making it altogether less comforting. Sam Bell's work-and-reward trajectory mirrors that offered by religion – work hard (and suffer) during life on Earth and be rewarded in the afterlife of Heaven.

Instead, in reality, when the body dies so does the mind and the personality, just as each iteration of Sam Bell is ultimately incinerated, denying him his promised reward. Gerty's programmed role to 'help' Sam in any way he can sees the robot become an unwitting accomplice in the demolition of Sam Bell's world view. Even Gerty makes a sacrifice in the end, though. In being rebooted to cover up Sam 2's escape, Gerty deletes 15 years of accumulated memories and experiences. It is wiped clean, losing learning from experience gained: artificial intelligence relies upon the ability to reason and evaluate based upon past experience. This is not a 'death' (the end of physical existence), but at least a loss of identity (comparable to that suffered by those with Alzheimer's or dementia). Does Gerty's willing self-sacrifice make up for compliance with Lunar Industries clone deception?

Essentially, Gerty functions as reason, teamed with Sam's own curiosity and investigation, so prioritising a scientific view of the world, rather than a religious one. Sam doesn't wait around for an all-knowing benevolent God to rescue him and change his situation. Presented with the challenge of his identical clone, he gets on and does it for himself. There is ultimately no reward awaiting Sam Bell, either on Earth or in heaven. There are simply more questions.

Sam Bell's faith in his own uniqueness is shattered by the events of *Moon*. The theology weaved throughout continually relates back to the film's central thematic concern: what constitutes a human? Gerty notices the changes in Sam even before his clone arrives, suggesting when cutting his hair: 'You don't seem like yourself today'. At that point, Sam is contemplating the end of his three years of service and his return home. He is just beginning to be troubled by hallucinations that suggest something is not right with his world. By the end, when Gerty is seeing off Sam 2, the robotic assistant exclaims: 'I hope life on Earth is everything you remember it to be.' Once again, memory is central to Sam's human core – his understanding of himself is of a man built from his memories. His identity does not rely upon faith (in Lunar Industries) but in himself. Ultimately, Sam's sense of identity (for both clones) is definitively established in Sam 2's final line to Gerty: 'We're not programmed. We're people.'

Notes

1. https://www.biblestudy.org/bibleref/meaning-of-numbers-in-bible/3.html.
2. Farah Mendhelsohn, 'Religion and Science Fiction' in Edward James & Farah Mendhelsohn (eds), *The Cambridge Companion to Science Fiction* (Cambridge: Cambridge University Press, 2003), 264-75.
3. Leo Casey, 'Questions, Curiosity, and the Inquiry Cycle', *E-Learning and Digital Media*, 11.5 (2014).
4. William James, 'The Moral Philosopher and the Moral Life', *International Journal of Ethics*, 1.3 (April 1891).
5. Henry Little, 'For All Mankind: A Brief Cultural History of the Moon', *The White Review* (September 2013) https://www.thewhitereview.org/feature/for-all-mankind-a-brief-cultural-history-of-the-moon/.

Chapter Five: 'We are not programmed!'

Duncan Jones concluded *Moon* with the statement from Sam 2 that 'We are not programmed', yet his films following *Moon* have showed a consistency of theme despite their vast disparity in style and approach, suggesting that somewhere deep within Jones' own 'programming' there is a core set of ideas he is inevitably fated to explore. Where *Moon* explored questions of identity surrounding the repeated re-creation of an individual, his follow-up, 2011's *Source Code*, instead saw the situation – the discovery of and attempt to defuse a bomb on a commuter train – repeated and re-created. This chapter explores the critical reaction to *Moon*, how Jones used that success to make a trio of diverse movies, and looks at how issues of parenthood and his relationship with his own father, David Bowie, and his work affected Jones' own approaches to making movies.

Moon was made for under $5 million, putting it firmly into the category of low-budget British filmmaking. Over its 30-week limited release in the US (at its height the film was playing in 252 theatres; blockbuster and wide-release movies can play on up to 3000 screens), *Moon* managed to gross almost exactly the same sum: $5,010,163. The international release almost doubled the box office take, adding a further $4,749,944 for a global full-release take of $9,760,107 (all figures from Box Office Mojo). The domestic UK box office took in just over £700,000 (according to Screen Rush). Additional revenues came from DVD and Blu-ray releases, as well as VOD releases internationally, making the film an undoubted success story.

Moon boasted high scores from aggregator review site *Rotten Tomatoes*, with a 90% rating from critics' reviews (although counting just 'top critics' that falls to 76%) and an almost matching 89% audience score (based upon over 100,000 audience ratings). While audiences expressed their appreciation by buying tickets, critics had to weigh up the film as part of the current (2009) movie marketplace and to explore its place in film history.

Writing in *Sight & Sound*, Philip Kemp labelled Jones' movie 'old-fashioned' but 'in the best sense: far more psychological drama than space opera … harking back to subtler, more ideas-driven entries in the genre such as *Solaris*, *Silent Running*, and *Dark Star*.' Kemp locates much of the film's success in Sam Rockwell's performance as the multiple Sam Bells. 'The acting burden falls on the shoulders of Rockwell, whose everyman quality and non-movie star looks make him ideal casting ... Rockwell skilfully differentiates the two cloned personae ... while never losing sight of them as two aspects of the same person. It's a tour-de-force to rank with Jeremy Irons' *Dead Ringers*. ... Jones rightly expends most of his SFX budget on making the interplay between them convincing, especially when they're fighting or playing ping pong.' As well as performance and character, Kemp also drew attention to the film's low-key production design, describing the Sarang moon base interior as 'appropriately low-tech and lived-in'. Besides the inter-personal relationships between the two Sams and the initially ambivalent-seeming character of Gerty, Kemp also touched upon the background politics of *Moon*. 'There's a hint of a political message – the way big corporations chew up their workers and spit them out – but Nathan Parker's script never rams it home ... the overall mood ... is melancholy rather than angry.' Kemp concluded by predicting an interesting filmmaking future for Jones: '[He] has made an intelligent, individual feature debut; on the strengths of this, he'll be one to watch.'

Other British reviews took a similar approach. Cosmo Landesman in the *Times Literary Supplement* noted that '*Moon* is a gripping sci-fi tale, but also has a lot of heart and humanity', while in *Empire*, Simon Crook celebrated the fact that 'They do make 'em like they used to – a fresh blast of old school sci-fi bursting with ideas and a stellar turn from Rockwell'. Connecting the film with the 1969 moon landing anniversary (just as Jones had intended), *The Guardian*'s critic Peter Bradshaw positioned *Moon* within a nostalgic discourse that included the screen science fiction of the past as well as the real-life achievement. 'The moon landing anniversary has been a time of nostalgia, for the glorious missions themselves and for the elegant, speculative and subversive sci-fi classics they inspired on screen in the next decade: *2001: A Space Odyssey*, *Solaris*, *Dark Star*, and *Silent Running*. ... The strength of *Moon* is also, paradoxically, its weakness: its evocation of loneliness and the vast, silent reaches of outer space. ... Rockwell is very good, and it is nice to see a major role for a distinctive and engaging performer. As for the director, this smart little picture is a very serviceable launch pad.'

For Tim Robey, writing in the *Daily Telegraph*, the nostalgic connection was to an American 1960s television series rather than to the intellectual big screen science fiction of the 1970s: '[Until the end *Moon*] remains crisp and unpredictable, but it does have the feel of an addictive *Outer Limits* episode finding ways to stretch itself over feature-length.' The UK *Time Out* labelled *Moon* a '1970s sci-fi throwback' that was 'unusually thoughtful, good-looking and well-acted. … Jones has created a credible theatre in which to stage a meditative play on isolation and identity within the bounds of wild fiction, the edges of which are curiously blurred. Less is more in Jones' eye: he knows that big ideas can be lost amid noisy gestures so keeps his drama within the confines of a few rooms, with only the odd, more poetic moment unfolding outside on the moon's surface.'

The British science journal *New Scientist* offered a unique take on the film. '*Moon* is not an eye-popping, special-effects bonanza. But it is arguably even more transportive – a lean, intense rumination on the effects of isolation, the depths of corporate depravity, and the nature of individuality. … The film masterfully transforms the lunar landscape from the joyful playground of Apollo days into a barren, industrial outpost.' Unlike most reviews, *New Scientist* engaged with the scientific reality of *Moon*. 'This vision of corporate corruption is … also its most unrealistic touch. Lunar Industries seems to have outfitted their base with enough supplies – and spare Sams – for many decades of work. It's hard to imagine this would be cheaper than training and sending workers from Earth every three years. A minor detail – gravity – isn't given consistent treatment. When outfitted in his spacesuit, Sam bounds with a slow-motion gait that matches the environment on the moon, whose gravity is one-sixth as strong as that on Earth. Back on the base, though, he walks as if he were on Earth. But this is a minor transgression. *Moon* is a stirring vision, and it will linger long after most big-budget sci-fi confections have faded from mind.'

The non-blockbuster nature of the film proved an attraction for other British critics. 'With its measured pacing, melancholy tone and eye for prosaic details, *Moon* is very different from the glossy sci-fi blockbuster, and far more satisfying,' wrote Wendy Ide in *The Times*, while for veteran critic Derek Malcolm, writing in the *London Evening Standard*, 'Jones, as writer and director, has fashioned a good-looking, claustrophobic piece despite his limited resources'. There were some negative reviews from British critics. Nigel Andrews in the *Financial Times* had no time at all for *Moon*, writing it off as nothing more than 'Psychedelic sci-fi' that suggested 'Glam rock goes off world' concluding Jones and Rockwell's efforts were 'wordy and overwrought, like a radio play in space.' For *Little White Lies*, however, the film's local origins were to be celebrated: 'This is a defiantly British film. It's one we can be proud of – in moderation.'

The real test of this low-key, low-budget British film's success came when it was screened for American critics, more used to big budget sci-fi blockbusters in the *Star Wars* (1977) or *Transformers* (2009) vein. How would *Moon* fare away from the indulgence of its 'home team' critics? In Hollywood trade paper *Variety*, Dennis Harvey summed up *Moon*: 'Despite its handsome look, the story stretches a bit thin over feature length.' Going into greater detail, Harvey saw *Moon* as lacking key elements. 'The questions surrounding Sam Bell's essential nature 'aren't played out in especially suspenseful or surprising fashion by director or scribe ... *Moon* actually gets a little dull in the later reels, just when it should be peaking in mystery and tension. There's not quite enough complexity of incident or character development here.' For the *Hollywood Reporter*, *Moon* was a 'well-made generic science fiction' film 'darkened by its own excellencies: The white, claustrophobic look and dark scopings are apt and moody, but a lack of physical action enervates the story thrust. Despite that, though, [the] sharp, individualistic dialogue is a quantum leap above the usual sci-fi drivel and should engage those who usually mock the genre as nerd stuff. ... Under Duncan Jones' kinetic direction, *Moon* also shines on the production front: Cinematographer Gary Shaw's shaded shots intensify the drama, and Clint Mansell's music heightens the psycho-scape.'

Other American critics were more outwardly enthusiastic. Writing in the *Chicago Sun-Times*, Roger Ebert said: '*Moon* is a superior example of that threatened genre, hard science-fiction, which is often about the interface between humans and alien intelligence of one kind of or other, including digital. ... The movie is really all about ideas. It only seems to be about emotions. How real are our emotions, anyway? How real are we?' It was the ideas of *Moon* that also engaged A. O. Scott, writing in the *New York Times*. 'The film's ideas are interesting, but don't feel entirely worked out, and Rockwell's intriguingly strange performance (or performances) is left suspended, without the context that would give Sam's plight its full emotional and philosophical impact.' For *Rolling Stone*'s Peter Travers, *Moon* was nothing short of a 'mesmerising mind-bender' that 'sneaks up and hits you hard'. Jones and his team 'pull off sci-fi miracles on a $5 million shoestring. *Moon* is a potent provocation that relies on ideas instead of computer tricks to stir up excitement.'

For Owen Gleiberman in *Entertainment Weekly*, *Moon* featured a 'grimy industrial look, the future strip-mined of all romance or idealism … Jones does a technically imaginative job befitting the son of the man who fell to Earth.' Gleiberman ultimately concludes, however, that *Moon* is no more than a 'brooding science fiction trifle'.

As with Glieberman's reference to David Bowie's appearance in Nic Roeg's *The Man Who Fell to Earth* (1976), many reviewers, particularly those in America, could not resist the temptation to point out that Duncan Jones was Bowie's son or to work in some other Bowie song-related joke or pun to their review. So it was with J. Hoberman's ultimately negative review of the film in the *Village Voice*: 'Impressively pulled together on a modest budget, *Moon* has a strong lead and a valid philosophical premise but, despite Bell's fissured psyche, the drama is inert. Ground control to Major Tom: *Moon* orbits an idea, but it doesn't go anywhere.' For the *Los Angeles Times*, Jones' film seemed to abandon its viewers: 'The film struggles to find entertainment within the esoteric. While they're trying to figure it out, we're left stranded on the dark side of the moon.'

The first time Duncan Jones saw *Moon* with a public audience was at the Sundance Film Festival in Utah in January 2009. It had been only a year since the project began shooting for a mere 33 days, followed by the week-long intricate model shoot, then months of post-production that involved adding the visual effects, putting together the sound mix, and recording Clint Mansell's score. For any film, especially for a low budget British movie, a single year's turnaround from first day of shooting to premier would be a major achievement; for a film that required the creation of entirely unreal imaginary environments (*Moon* couldn't simply shoot on the streets of London), it seemed an almost impossible task, yet Jones and his collaborators achieved it.

Being such an unknown quality – first time, unheard of director, oddball science fiction, low budget – *Moon* had encountered some difficulties in securing a distributor, especially in the United States. Producer Stuart Fenegan pitched the project around all the big hitters, with Sony coming onboard in May 2008, securing worldwide release rights and offering the project the money required to complete the film's financing package. The Sundance screening created such a buzz that Fenegan was approached about distribution rights by distributors who'd previously passed on the project. For them it was too late, the Sony deal had already been done (out of necessity) and the filmmakers lost the chance to auction their film to the highest bidder in a competitive marketplace.

What the Sundance screening did achieve was to begin building a critical buzz. That convinced Sony to seriously consider a theatrical release, as there had earlier been some thought that *Moon* might have gone straight to DVD. A roll-out at other major festivals – Tribeca in April 2009 and Edinburgh in June 2009 – helped convince Sony to schedule *Moon* for a June 2009 US release. The film opened in New York and Los Angeles, securing reviews from all the major publications, before hitting other major US cities. The UK had to wait until July 2009 to see the homegrown hit, followed by an Australian release in October. By the end of the year, *Moon* was appearing on many critics lists as one of the year's most outstanding films.

Positive reviews and decent box office are the fundamental feedback that offers filmmakers approbation, but awards ultimately stroke their egos. Jones was awarded a BAFTA for Outstanding Debut by a British Writer, Director or Producer, while his team of producers, including Fenegan and Trudie Styler, were also nominated. The British Independent Film Awards declared *Moon* to be the Best British Independent Film of the year and Jones won the Douglas Hickox Award for Best Debut Director. The Edinburgh International Film Festival also declared *Moon* to be the Best New British Feature of 2009. Several other festivals and critics circles also garlanded *Moon* with awards, with several recognising Sam Rockwell for his unique contribution.

Being science fiction, the film also scooped several genre-focused awards, including the Hugo for Best Dramatic Presentation – Long Form, and Best Horror or Science Fiction Film from the Internet Film Critic Society. There was a clean sweep for *Moon* at the Sitges Catalonian International Film Festival (which focuses on genre fare) with the film scoring Best Actor, Best Director, Best Production Design (Tony Noble) and

Best Screenplay (Nathan Parker). Parker, with Jones, scored again, winning Best First Feature-Length Film Screenplay from the Writers' Guild of Great Britain. Needless to say, such a low-budget, genre-based, British production did not trouble that year's Hollywood Oscars.

Almost as soon as word had got out from Sundance about *Moon*, there was interest from American agents and studios in what Duncan Jones and his team were planning next. Fenegan recognised the need to move quickly to capitalise upon the 'hot streak' that *Moon* provided, hoping that he and Jones could get a new movie into production within a year of *Moon*'s debut. Although Jones had his 'passion project' of *Mute* ready-scripted, the pair came to a view that the ambitious story they hoped to tell was not right for their sophomore effort. *Mute* would need to be worked up to creatively and in terms of winning bigger budgets. The ideal project, Fenegan recognised, would be something more cinematically ambitious than *Moon*, so with a bigger budget, but which also contained the same 'intellectual sci-fi' approach, seeing that as a possible Jones–Fenegan cinematic trademark.

Shortly after *Moon*'s success both Jones and Fenegan relocated to the world's centre of popular filmmaking, Los Angeles, and quickly signed with Creative Artists Agency (CAA). One of the agency's acting clients, Jake Gyllenhaal, had seen *Moon* and was keen to work with Jones. The pair hit it off at a casual meeting, while Fenegan searched for suitable scripts that might hook Gyllenhaal's commitment. Gyllenhaal was no stranger to sci-fi, having made an impression with 2001's *Donnie Darko*, and with appearances in environmental disaster blockbuster *The Day After Tomorrow* (2004) and the computer-game inspired *Prince of Persia: The Sands of Time* (2010).

Source Code originated in a spec script sold by Ben Ripley to Universal in 2007, before Duncan Jones had even begun work on *Moon*. The script made that year's 'black list' of hot unproduced screenplays. Ripley told the Writers' Guild of America that 'I had a suspicion that if I got this right, it could really open a new level for my writing career.'[1] Gyllenhaal was already attached to Ripley's script, but a suitable director had not yet been found.

Fenegan recognised a potent mix of genres in Ripley's script, describing it as combining body-hopping television series *Quantum Leap* (1989–93, 2022–), *The Hurt*

Locker (2008), and *RoboCop* (1987). Jones was signed as director with Gyllenhaal's approval. *Source Code* was a major step up for Jones with a budget of $32 million, six times as large as that for *Moon*, allowing for a greater scope of cinematic action and more assured visual effects than on the earlier film.

Although not written by him nor directly developed for him, Duncan Jones would have been hard-pressed to find a more suitable and thematically resonant follow-up to *Moon* than *Source Code*. Where *Moon* was centrally concerned with the repeated recreation of the individual, *Source Code* depicted a situation (the finding and defusing of a bomb on a commuter train) that is repeated and recreated through various iterations. One of the signs that defines an auteur filmmaker is repeated thematic concerns and narrative repetition in subsequent projects.

Each film features a lone protagonist (in Sam Bell and Colter Stevens) confronted by revelations about their true identities (Sam's a clone; Colter's near death, reliving the same eight minutes). Each film sees the protagonist engaged in a proxy conflict with a distant and bureaucratic organisation (Lunar Industries in *Moon*; the military and scientists in *Source Code*) that are ultimately responsible for his plight. Each protagonist has help from a supportive figure from within the organisations (Gerty, the robotic assistant in *Moon*; Captain Goodwin [Vera Farmiga] in *Source Code*). In shaping *Source Code* so explicitly to follow the tropes and themes of *Moon*, Duncan Jones was engaged in the repetition and recreation that he puts both lead characters through. They are 'someone ... abused by the system that they are there to work for, and not being given all the information. Feeling alienated by their job, and the circumstances that they're in.'[2]

Jones sites both of these narratives in the familiar and everyday. In *Moon*, Sam Bell has a simple job to do – supervising and maintaining the Helium-3 harvesters – that no doubt consists of many repeated everyday tasks, probably working through a checklist. He's an ordinary guy, a 'blue collar' American worker (albeit one working solo on the moon), depicted in the same style as a 'roughneck' oil rig worker. He is introduced in an unkempt and dishevelled state, with an unruly beard and a scruffy baseball cap. The fact of living and working on the moon is treated as mundane as any other blue collar factory job on Earth – it's a task that needs to be done, and

Moon

Sam Bell is doing it for the pay day. The disruption to his world comes in the shape of Sam's accident and the activation of a replacement clone, resulting in there being two of him on the moon.

Source Code opens in a similarly mundane location: a morning commuter train heading into Chicago from the suburbs. The disruption here is more immediate – upon waking Colter Stevens (Gyllenhaal) doesn't know where he is or who he is; even his face reflected in a mirror doesn't match that which he expects to see. The surroundings and activities he experiences are everyday 'normal', but his cognition of this world is not. The first mystery he has to solve is that of his own identity, essentially the same problem confronted by Sam Bell when he meets his duplicate. The narrative drive of both movies, in their opening half-hour or so, is to explore and explain the mystery of the exact nature of the lead characters.

For Sam Bell, the revelation that he is just one of many identical clones, all with the same memories and personalities upon wakening, is the disruptive incident that dramatically changes his world and his perception of reality. For Colter Stevens, his second awakening within what appears to be some kind of life-support pod (modelled after his helicopter cockpit in Afghanistan) and his journey back into the 'source code' is when he faces the unreality of his situation and is confronted by the fact that the world he sees is not the world as it actually is. Where Sam Bell has, across a period of a decade or more, been killed and recreated, so Colter Stevens undergoes the same process but in a much more condensed time period, an eight-minute repeating loop. Much of the earlier parts of *Source Code* play out in near real time, so Stevens returns to the same eight minutes, trying each time to progress his 'story arc' of discovering and defusing the bomb. His situation is repeated and recreated, just as Sam Bell himself has been recreated so he can repeatedly carry out his tasks.

The only way both protagonists in *Moon* and *Source Code* can escape their situations is by breaking this pattern of repetition and recreation. Once past the initial strangeness of their concurrent existence, the two Sam Bells team up to work out a way one of them can escape Sarang base and return to Earth, so revealing Lunar Industries' deception. Once Colter Stevens has a handle on his mission, the only way to escape the eight minutes he is trapped in is to find the bomb and the terrorist perpetrator in order to avoid the explosion and so save the passengers. This, in turn, allows him to escape his half-life state and finally die (while also living on in a parallel universe).

Given that *Source Code* came to him, rather than being originated by him as *Moon* was, it is evident that Duncan Jones took the material available and reshaped to better suit his auteurist thematic concerns. Both *Moon* and *Source Code* depend upon a fusion of their narrative styles and their themes. They are episodic in nature, and follow linear narrative plots, while at the same time repeating scenes and situations as a method of progressing the story. In both, a single human life is abused for the benefit of the greater good (so re-enacting the scapegoat bargain). There's one other neat repetition in *Source Code* which directly references *Moon* – Christina (Michelle Monaghan), a fellow passenger Colter encounters on the train, has a ringtone on her phone. It is, of course, 'The One and Only' by Chesney Hawkes.

While a critical hit, *Source Code* was an average performer at the box office. The US take totalled $54.7 million, with international receipts adding a further $92.6 million for a global total take of $147.3 million. The combination of Ripley's tricksy script with Gyllenhaal's driven performance and Jones' light-touch direction made *Source Code* a hit with most critics. 'It's Jones' restrained direction that keeps *Source Code* moving, and confirms him as the rare filmmaker able ... to understand that even movies with explosions don't have to be dumb to entertain,' said the online *A.V. Club*. Because the film played with similar conceptual science-fiction ideas to *Moon*, it was often compared with Jones' debut, albeit as more of a puzzle and perhaps less emotionally engaging. *Film Comment* magazine noted 'Jones ... has a light touch of the sort that enlivens the material without trivialising it', while the *Independent* said that Jones 'ran similar rings around consciousness in his acclaimed debut, *Moon*. The great gimmick of this new film is its licence to thrill.' The repeating scenario drew some comparisons to *Groundhog Day* (1993), while the high-tech reality warping nature of the plot saw some critics recalling Jones' mentor Tony Scott's *Deja Vu* (2006). For the *San Francisco Chronicle*, Jones had used *Source Code* not to foreground 'splashy special effects, but as a doorway into the human soul'.

After the double whammy success of *Moon* and *Source Code*, Jones took a creative and critical tumble with *Warcraft* (2016), based on the popular video game. Originally announced a decade earlier in May 2006, the film had undergone various permutations of writers and directors before Jones got involved. Among the suggested directors were the notorious Uwe Boll (the *BloodRayne* series) and Sam Raimi (the 2002–7 *Spider-Man* trilogy), before Jones was signed up to direct in 2013. Jones immediately tossed out the existing script, feeling it was too black and white in depicting the human characters as the good guys and the orcs as evil. During production, Jones had a series of personal troubles, including his wife Rodene Ronquillo's diagnosis with breast cancer and the death of his father, David Bowie, in January 2016. 'My film started and ended with cancer,'[3] Jones said to the *New York Times* of his troubled time making *Warcraft*.

It was all the more disappointing for Jones, then, when *Warcraft* crashed and burned at the box office, failing to provide the launch pad for an anticipated film franchise. The $160 million dollar movie grossed just over $47 million at the domestic US box office. It was saved from total failure by a respectable international box office take of almost $392 million for a global final total of $439 million. *The Hollywood Reporter* suggested that *Warcraft* had to reach at least $450 million at the global box office to secure a sequel. As it was, the magazine reported, the film carried a loss of anywhere between $15 million and $40 million, when promotional and marketing costs were added. *Warcraft* became, however, the highest grossing film based on a video game, knocking *Source Code* star Jake Gyllenhaal's *Prince of Persia: The Sands of Time* off the top spot.

Critically, *Warcraft* was also a washout. Several reviews noted that Jones was perhaps not the right director for such expansive and overblown material, better suited to the more intimate tales of *Moon* and *Source Code*. While the *New York Times* damned the movie with faint praise by simply declaring it 'watchable', *Rolling Stone* stated it was 'mostly worthless'. The UK's *Empire* magazine slated *Warcraft* as 'empty and impenetrable', while the online *A.V. Club* commented 'Rarely is so much time, money, and cutting-edge technology expended on a spectacle so devoid of wonder'. The problem for many, especially those not fans of the video game, was that the mythology of the world of *Warcraft* proved to be difficult to get to grips with. Jones wanted to avoid the good vs. evil simplicity of Tolkien's *The Lord of the Rings*, but for a summer blockbuster entertainment with wide appeal that straight forward approach would seem the right one. Many of the reviewers nonetheless went to great lengths to suggest the failure of *Warcraft* should not prevent Jones from continuing to make films. As Peter Travers, of *Rolling Stone*, noted: 'Duncan Jones will live to fight another day.'

Jones did, indeed, live to fight again, retreating from *Warcraft* to finally realise the project he'd been nursing for a decade and a half – he decided the time was now right for *Mute* (2018). As well as being positioned as a 'spiritual successor' to *Moon*, the film would reunite much of the *Moon* production team with Jones, including producer Stuart Fenegan, cinematographer Gary Shaw, and composer Clint Mansell. 'I was unwilling to let it go,' said Jones of *Mute*. Jones found the only way he could get his film produced was to work with streaming service Netflix, rather than one of the traditional studios. 'The studios don't make these kinds of films [anymore], they're focused on making big budget, opening weekend movies that must be as effective as possible with all four quadrants. This new wave of being able to get films made that are different types of movies and different genres is because of places like Netflix and Amazon and Apple.'[4] The deal with Netflix offered Jones 'final cut', something he'd rarely enjoyed since *Moon*, but there were compromises inherent in making a movie for a streaming service. 'The con side is it's not going to have a big theatrical [release], which is a shame because I'd love people to be able to see it together on a big screen. This was the only way that this film was going to get made.'[5]

Starring Alexander Skarsgård as a mute bartender searching a near-future Berlin for his missing girlfriend, *Mute* debuted on Netflix in February 2018. Originally, before completing *Moon*, Jones had thought of *Mute* as a straight-ahead London-set gangster film. It was only later that he recast it in a science-fiction light, relocating the story to Berlin, circa 2050. Wearing its *Blade Runner* (1982) inspirations a little too clearly, *Mute* met a largely hostile critical reception. *Empire* was brutal in its summing up: 'Fans of *Moon* and *Source Code* be warned – *Mute* is sadly, almost tragically, not worth the wait.' For many critics, the visuals were impressive, while the characters and narrative were derivative and disappointing. 'Early trailers made it look like a neon-noir cross between *Blade Runner* and *The Fifth Element* (1997). Sadly, it's just another airless dud,' said *Entertainment Weekly*. The *Hollywood Reporter* claimed: 'The narrative doesn't quite coalesce, and except for a few late moments, it doesn't deliver the grim, indelible shivers of the best noir.' For *Variety*, the director's latest work was disappointing in the context of his earliest films. 'What is Jones trying to say with *Mute*? One would hardly guess this over-congested generic exercise came from the same mind as the elegant, almost minimalistic *Moon*, which made far better use of all that went unsaid.'

Beyond the critical response, *Mute* established itself as inhabiting the same filmic universe as *Moon*. During a diner scene, a background television is showing the hearings that followed Sam 2's return to Earth. Sam Rockwell reconnected with Duncan Jones to make an uncredited cameo, moving forward the saga of the Sams. While two Sam clones get to speak, many more are pictured sitting in the audience, while a scrolling caption indicates that all the remaining 156 Sam Bell clones that Lunar Industries had stashed on the moon have been repatriated to Earth. 'That was always going to be the way we linked it to *Moon*,' confirmed Jones. 'We had a lot of fun that day. Sam came out to Berlin just for the day to do it. [He] performed all of his various parts. It was actually kind of nice, because it had been a pretty somber, hard shoot.'[6] The Sam Bell character also features on a background poster in *Mute* that demands his/their freedom.

Thematically, Jones also saw *Moon* and *Mute* were not only connected, both to each other but also to his own life. '*Moon* was about facing different perspectives of yourself and how you saw the world at different times. I had that experience on *Mute*. I saw the project one way 16 years ago, and it has evolved dramatically over that decade and a half,'[7] said Jones.

The plan for a *Moon–Mute* film trilogy with a yet unmade third film, focusing on a road trip taken by two sisters, looks unlikely to be completed, at least as films. Jones attempted to get the female-driven *Moon* spin-off made after *Source Code*, but couldn't attract any studio interest. 'They're all coming out in the wrong order,' claimed Jones, highlighting that he wanted to make *Mute* first, while *Moon* was a product of necessity. That same approach had to be adopted to complete the *Moon* trilogy.

By 2020, Jones had settled on telling the final part of his now multi-media story through the medium of the graphic novel. As his tale had grown in the telling, he realised he'd need a *Warcraft*-sized budget to do the story justice on film, and that was unlikely to happen. There were, however, other ways of telling stories. Entitled *Madi: Once Upon a Time in the Future*, the 260-page graphic novel final 'Moonivese' instalment was co-written with novelist Alex De Campi and illustrated by multiple artists. Funded through a Kickstarter appeal, the £40,000 project raised over £125,000 within hours from committed *Moon* and *Mute* fans who wanted to see the final part of the puzzle. 'Film is just one way to tell a story,'[8] Jones told the *Guardian*. Madi, the title character, is an 'enhanced' ex-military operative previously indentured to one of the world's huge corporations as a mercenary, a role that allows her to pay off the cost of the bio-tech she's had installed. Rejecting her position in a corrupt society, Madi rebels. In the light of Jones' next planned film, she could be described as some kind of 'rogue trooper'.

Across the decade since *Moon*, Duncan Jones had made sure to keep his momentum going. With both *Moon* and *Source Code* establishing him as a director of smart, high-concept science-fiction entertainment, the set-backs of *Warcraft* and, to a lesser extent, of *Mute*, did little to slow his momentum. There were several unmade or planned projects that Jones could return to: a planned Second World War submarine thriller *Escape from the Deep*; an Ian Fleming bio-pic, with a screenplay by Matthew Brown based upon book *The Man Behind James Bond* by Andrew Lycett, which was supported by the Fleming estate (maybe positioning Jones as a future James Bond director); and the planned adaptation of Tony Kent's 2018 novel *Killer Intent* as a television series.

In the wake of *Mute*, Jones was soon deep into development of a movie based upon the *2000AD* comic book character Rogue Trooper. Created by Gerry Finley-Day and Dave Gibbons and debuting in 1981, *Rogue Trooper* followed the adventures of a genetically engineered, blue skinned near-indestructible super soldier who sported a trademark mohican haircut. While tackling a similar property with a comic book or video game source as *Warcraft* might seem risky for Jones, the return to a UK-based production (with *2000AD* owners Rebellion establishing a $100 million studio facility for *Rogue Trooper* and their other comic book assets) was a welcome development in Jones' filmmaking trajectory. A return to the high concept yet emotionally engaging approach of both *Moon* and *Source Code* with the comic book sensibilities of *Rogue Trooper* feels like a recipe for revived cinematic success.

A man is alone in a high-tech environment that he is responsible for maintaining. He is aided by a trio of robotic companions. He is hiding a perilous secret, but even he may not be truly aware of his actual real-world status or true identity. That may sound like a garbled plot synopsis of Duncan Jones' *Moon*, but it is instead a summary of Gavin Rothery's directorial debut, 2020's *Archive*. The prime mover behind the look of *Moon*'s Sarang base essentially remixed many of the elements that made *Moon* such a success a decade on with his own film. The primary link between *Moon* and *Archive* is the minimalist aesthetic, but there are many other connections, some cleverly hidden.

Archive follows artificial intelligence scientist George Almore (Theo James), who is several years into a research project following the death of his wife Jules (Stacy Martin) in a car accident. Almore works in a largely white facility, code-named The Garden, atop a remote mountain in Kyoto, where he has two boxy robots housing his previous attempts at creating a functioning AI (these robots are clearly siblings of *Moon*'s Gerty in design and execution). Almore has an ulterior motive in pursuing his research – he hopes to eventually house the hard drive-stored consciousness of his dead wife in a humanoid robot, thereby bringing her back to 'life'. He is, however, in a race against the clock as her archived human consciousness is slowly decaying.

There is so much in *Archive*, both written and directed by Rothery, that echoes Jones' *Moon*. From the mostly lone protagonist with a secret (and another, unknown even to him) to the remote scientific base location and the boxy prototype AI robots, it all feels very familiar. Rothery innovates in the twist that concludes the movie. Sporadic communication between the living Almore and his dead wife's stored consciousness is possible through halting phone calls, and several are depicted. At the film's conclusion it is revealed that George is actually the one who is dead, and his experiences are part of a post-life simulation that is slowly winding down. His wife, Jules, is alive in the real world, raising their daughter while saying goodbye to the digitally stored personality of her husband as it blinks out of existence. Combining the existential drama of *Moon* with its clean-lined design aesthetics, Rothery produced a spiritual sequel to Jones' film.

Archive originated not long after *Moon*. Rothery was inspired by the simultaneous failure of several hard drives that contained much of his archived art work, including work he'd completed for *Moon*. Wondering why his devices had failed, he conceived of an artificial intelligence that, as soon as it becomes 'conscious', simply wants to kill itself. The story evolved, but it took the better part of the next decade to line up the financing. Of the ultimate design aesthetic, Rothery was happy to admit: 'I was really leaning into the approach I devised for *Moon*, so this whole endeavour for me was quite straight forward as I already had a working template. I'd already had some success with Gerty, so I felt confident going in that I could expand on that without too much danger. It was really all about ... keeping the focus on the characters rather than trying to show off with the visuals.'[9]

Archive was an extension of those same 1970s science-fiction movies that had so inspired *Moon*. Where Duncan Jones had moved beyond that work with *Source Code*, *Warcraft*, and *Mute*, Rothery seemed content to further explore the themes and aesthetic of thoughtful 1970s science fiction on a budget. Both *Moon* and *Archive* came from the same roots, but in his filmmaking *Moon*'s Duncan Jones has grown beyond the limitations of low-budget British filmmaking to embrace blockbuster American entertainment, albeit with mixed results. Jones' planned film of *2000AD*'s *Rogue Trooper* may see the director adopting the best of both worlds, mixing low-budget British filmmaking know-how with high ambition American-style blockbuster entertainment.

It may seem reductive to search the work of Duncan Jones for echoes of that of his father, David Bowie. However, this task is undertaken not to diminish the creative endeavour of either individual but in the hope of illuminating the work of both. It simply cannot be denied that there are concrete (if most likely unconscious) echoes, parallels, and developments of the work of the father in the movies created by the son. After all, as Wordsworth (or was it the Beach Boys?) had it in his 1802 poem 'My Heart Leaps Up': 'The child is the father of the man'.

Beyond his pathbreaking music, Bowie also had a strong creative presence in film.

One of his earliest acting roles came as the inspirational muse figure of 'The Boy' in one of British director Michael Armstrong's early shorts, *The Image* (1969). This role came in parallel with Bowie establishing his musical presence with his first charting single, 'Space Oddity' (at #5 in the UK pop charts) that same year of 1969, paving the way for his 1970s success. It was Nic Roeg's selection of Bowie to play the alien Thomas Jerome Newton in his 1976 film of Walter Tevis' novel *The Man Who Fell to Earth* that defined Bowie's screen persona. It and subsequent films drew upon Bowie's real-life oddness, notably his appearance in the documentaries *Ziggy Stardust and the Spiders From Mars* (1973) and *Cracked Actor* (1975). Androgynous and separate from the rest of mankind, Bowie's screen characters in the 1980s alone ran the gamut from a vampire in *The Hunger* (Tony Scott, 1983), a conflicted soldier in *Merry Christmas, Mr. Lawrence* (1983), a 1950s pop star in *Absolute Beginners* (1986), and Jareth the Goblin King in *Labyrinth* (1986).

Bowie harboured ambitions of becoming a film director himself. He selected filmmakers to work with from whom he felt he could learn, including Roeg and Martin Scorsese in *The Last Temptation of Christ* (1988). He developed ideas for full-length films based upon his work on albums like *The Rise and Fall of Ziggy Stardust and the Spiders from Mars* (1972) and *Diamond Dogs* (1974), even to the extent of creating detailed scale models and intricate storyboards of specific scenes. Bowie approached his musical work as an all-round creative endeavour, adopting the position of 'director'.

It was on the set of some of his father's films that the young Duncan Jones was first exposed to moviemaking, notably on *Labyrinth* and Tony Scott's *The Hunger*, where the then 11-year-old Jones was set loose with a camera. Bowie encouraged his son's endeavours, buying him a Super-8 camera and collaborating in the creation of short films featuring stop motion animated *Star Wars* action figures. Bowie's musical and cinematic explorations of misfits and outsiders would find further expression in Duncan Jones' film characters. His focus on isolated characters attempting to fix an impossible problem can't help but recall his own childhood, separated from his mother and often on the road with his self-obsessed rock star father.

That Jones' film debut should focus on an astronaut who ultimately cracks up, echoing his father's breakthrough song 'Space Oddity', should come as little surprise. The Lunar Industries promotional film that opens *Moon* asks the question 'Where are we now?', which not co-incidentally was the first title of the first single released from Bowie's 2013 album *The Next Day* (his first album for a decade, and as it turned out, his penultimate release). Further, Rockwell's Sam Bell has to reconstruct an essential self from the revelation that he is just one of many, just as Bowie as rock star was just one of many creative personas he adopted throughout the 1970s and 1980s. Both Bowie and Sam Bell apparently contained multitudes. By the end, Sam Bell has become 'the man who fell to Earth', returning to a 'home' he has never in reality experienced before. Bowie returned the creative compliment. His video for the single 'Blackstar' (directed by Johan Renck) opened with a seemingly dead astronaut (a shout out to Major Tom?) whose space suit is adorned with a decal or patch featuring a Gerty-like smiling face emoji symbol.

Of course, Jones denies that any such connections are deliberate. In an interview, when they were highlighted, he claimed these echoes to be 'totally unconscious'. He said of growing up with his father and their shared interest in space: 'I was surrounded by a lot of the similar things that were interesting him back in those early days, but to be honest when my dad was doing his space-themed work he was actually a helluva lot younger than I am doing mine. So I think we come from very different perspectives ... there was no direct referencing from me. It was just an interest in the same subject matter.' Sealing the deal was the performance in space of Bowie's song. Canadian astronaut Commander Chris Hadfield covered 'Space Oddity' while aboard the International Space Station in 2013, four years after the release of *Moon*. Bowie said that performance was 'possibly the most poignant version of the song ever created'.[10]

However, there is a parenting theme that runs throughout the filmic work of Duncan Jones, from *Moon* through to *Mute*, often focused on fathers and sons. Talking of his thematically-linked trilogy of *Moon*, *Mute*, and the unmade (except in graphic novel form) *Madi*, Jones said: 'They cover similar subject matter – autonomy, parenting, the kinds of things that interest me ...'[11] *Moon* features self-parenting, in which clone Sam 2 has to be the 'adult' educating the more distraught Sam 1 about their exact nature. Even Gerty might be regarded as a surrogate parental figure to Sam, in that he is responsible for running the moon base (the household), and does everything to aid Sam's healthy development (parenting). *Mute* similarly explores the theme of parenthood, primarily through the connection the protagonist Leo has with the little girl Josie (the largely ignored daughter of Paul Rudd's rogue surgeon 'Cactus' Bill), a character who like Leo never speaks and has been deprived of her voice. Like Leo, whose Amish parents refused the surgery that could have saved his voice, Josie suffers thanks to the actions or choices of a parent (just as the young Duncan Jones did – the film was dedicated to Bowie and Jones' late nanny Marion Skene). Of *Mute*, Jones said: 'An awful lot of the story revolves around the nature of parenthood. What makes a good parent?'[12] The film's central setting of a future Berlin was also clearly inspired by the time Jones spent with his father in the city in the 1970s. Even *Warcraft*, the very epitome of soulless big-budget blockbuster Hollywood filmmaking, was reshaped by Jones in a rewrite of the screenplay to feature issues of parenting, with subplots concerning fathers and sons, and a sympathetic orc couple preparing for the arrival of their first child (an experience Jones was shortly to share). The outsider theme, inspired by Bowie's work, turns up in *Warcraft*, as it does in *Moon*, *Source Code*, and *Mute*: Garona (Paula Patton), a half-Orc rejected by her own tribe but also rejected by the human forces, is an outsider in her own world trying to find a place where she belongs. The same thematic concerns can be applied to Sam Bell in *Moon*, Colter Stevens in *Source Code*, and Leo in *Mute* – all outsiders from the communities to which they find themselves attached.

Similarly, Duncan Jones is perhaps searching for a place where he belongs, cinematically speaking. His debut and sophomore efforts, *Moon* and *Source Code*, shared enough thematic and storytelling DNA to suggest that Jones was preparing to plough a furrow as a high-concept intelligent science-fiction auteur. Then he decided to play with the Hollywood 'big boys' with the would-be blockbuster *Warcraft*. Where *Moon* succeeded with its throwback practical models, *Warcraft* crashed and burned under a surfeit of ambition and CGI images that looked more like a video game someone else was playing rather than a movie (although the would-be auteur managed, even here, to replicate some of his thematic concerns). *Mute* was a retreat, of sorts; a long-held ambition realised, and a film that discomforted a nascent fan base that wasn't expecting such a dark narrative.

All of this had come from the seeds laid down in one movie: *Moon*. 'We put our body and soul into making that movie.' said Jones of his debut film. 'I don't think I could have put any more of myself into that movie than I did and, I think maybe in some ways the naivety and the innocence of us going into that film is probably one of the only reasons we were able to survive it. I think if we'd known how exhausting it was going to be, maybe we would've been a little less ambitious.'[13] That ambition carried Jones through not only *Moon* but each subsequent film. It took him a while to realise his calling as a filmmaker, and the work that has resulted is inevitably filled with resonances with Jones' childhood as the son of David Bowie. From 'Space Oddity' to Jones' own odyssey through space, his filmmaking ambitions lay not only with *Moon* but far beyond.

Notes

1. Denis Faye, 'Practice Makes Perfect', *Writers Guild of America* (October 2011).
2. Bryan Bishop, 'For the Horde', *The Verge* (no date) https://www.theverge.com/2016/6/7/11874342/duncan-jones-warcraft-movie-director-interview.
3. Dave Itzkoff, 'Duncan Jones, David Bowie's son, on Making Warcraft and Facing His Own Battles', *New York Times* (May 2016).
4. John Hazelton, 'Duncan Jones on Netflix thriller Mute', *Screen Daily* (March 2018) https://www.screendaily.com/features/duncan-jones-on-netflix-thriller-mute-i-was-unwilling-to-let-it-go/5126913.article.
5. Ibid.
6. Don Kaye, 'How Netflix's Mute Connects to Duncan Jones' Moon', *Den of Geek* (February 2018) https://www.denofgeek.com/movies/how-netflixs-mute-connects-to-duncan-jones-moon/.
7. Ryan Britt, 'Duncan Jones Explains Why *Mute* and *Moon* Had to Be Connected', *Inverse* (February 2018) https://www.inverse.com/article/41575-mute-moon-easter-eggs-duncan-jones-interview.
8. David Barnett, 'Film is just one way to tell a story: Duncan Jones on his comic book sequel to Moon', *The Guardian* (20 May 2020).
9. Jez Stoker, *Archive*: Interview with Film Writer/Director Gavin Rothery, BorrowingTape.com (no date) https://borrowingtape.com/interviews/archive-interview-film-writer-director-gavin-rothery.
10. Becky Ferreira, 'Chris Hadfield's song in space was no oddity', *New York Times* (2

November 2020).
11. Karen Han, 'Director Duncan Jones says the Finale to the *Moon* Trilogy will be an "Action Road Movie"', *Polygon* (2 July 2019), https://www.polygon.com/2019/7/12/20687928/moon-duncan-jones-interview-10th-anniversary.
12. Luke Morgan Britton, 'David Bowie Inspired His Son's New Film, *Mute*', *NME* (16 February 2018).
13. Matt Goldberg, 'Duncan Jones Reflects on Moon and What He Had Planned for a Warcraft Trilogy', *Collider* (July 2019), https://collider.com/duncan-jones-interview-moon-warcraft-rogue-trooper/#mute.

Bibliography & Works Cited

BOOKS

Bukatman, Scott, *Terminal Identity: The Virtual Subject in Postmodern Science Fiction* (Durham, NC: Duke University Press, 1993)

Disch, Thomas, *The Dreams Our Stuff is Made Of: How Science Fiction Conquered the World* (New York: Touchstone, 1998)

James, Edward & Farah Mendhelsohn (eds), *The Cambridge Companion to Science Fiction* (Cambridge: Cambridge University Press, 2003)

Pegg, Nicholas, *The Complete David Bowie*, 6th ed. (London: Titan Books, 2011)

Robb, Brian J., *Counterfeit Worlds: Philip K. Dick on Film* (London: Titan Books, 2005)

Roberts, Adam (ed.), *Science Fiction* (London and New York: Routledge, 2000)

Ward, Simon, *Making Moon: A British Sci-Fi Cult Classic* (London: Titan Books, 2019)

JOURNALS, PAPERS, & ARTICLES

Barnett, David, 'Film is just one way to tell a story: Duncan Jones on his comic book sequel to Moon', *The Guardian* (20 May 2020)

Bell, James John, 'Exploring the "Singularity"', *Futurist*, 37.3 (2003)

Berti, Agustín & Andrea Torrano, 'Duncan Jones' *Moon*: Do Clones Dream of Uncopyrighted Sheep?' *Jura Gentium Cinema* (2012)

Bishop, Bryan, 'For the Horde', *The Verge* (no date)

Boon, Mashya, 'Remarriage of the Self; Clones and Cavell', *Film–Philosophy Conference* (2016)

Brew, Simon, 'Duncan Jones Interview: The Man Who Made *Moon*', *Den of Geek* (November 2009)

Britt, Ryan, 'Duncan Jones Explains Why *Mute* and *Moon* Had to Be Connected', *Inverse* (February 2018)

Britton, Luke Morgan, 'David Bowie Inspired His Son's New Film, *Mute*', *NME* (16 February 2018)

Brown, Arnold, 'The Robotic Economy', *Futurist*, 40.4 (2006)

Casey, Leo, 'Questions, Curiosity, and the Inquiry Cycle', *E-Learning and Digital Media*, 11.5 (2014)

Erickson, Steve, 'Director Duncan Jones on Low-Budget Moon', *Studio Daily* (June 2009)

Faye, Denis, 'Practice Makes Perfect', *Writers Guild of America* (October 2011)

Ferreira, Becky, 'Chris Hadfield's song in space was no oddity', *New York Times* (2 November 2020)

Glancy, Graham D., and Erin L. Murray, 'The Psychiatric Aspects of Solitary Confinement.' *Victims & Offenders*, 1.4 (2006): 361–8

Goldberg, Matt, 'Duncan Jones Reflects on *Moon* and What He Had Planned for a *Warcraft* Trilogy', Collider (July 2019)

Graham, Caroline, 'Zowie Bowie: How a son of rock royalty survived a bitter rift with his mother to earn genuine success', *Mail on Sunday* (8 August 2009)

Grassian, Stuart, 'Neuropsychiatric Effects of Solitary Confinement: The trauma of psychological torture', *PsycINFO* (7 Nov. 2012)

Han, Karen, 'Director Duncan Jones says the Finale to the *Moon* Trilogy will be an "Action Road Movie"', *Polygon* (12 July 2019)

Haynes, Deborah J., 'On The Need For Ethical Aesthetics', *Art Journal*, 56.3 (1997)

Hazelton, John, 'Duncan Jones on Netflix thriller *Mute*', *Screen Daily* (March 2018)

Hutson, Matthew, 'Duncan Jones on the Moon', *Psychology Today* (July 2009)

Itzkoff, Dave, 'Duncan Jones and *Moon*: Major Tom's Son at Ground control', *New York Times* (3 June 2009)

Itzkoff, Dave, 'Duncan Jones, David Bowie's son, on Making *Warcraft* and Facing His Own Battles', *New York Times* (May 2016)

James, William, 'The Moral Philosopher and the Moral Life', *International Journal of Ethics*, 1.3 (April 1891)

Kaye, Don, 'How Netflix's *Mute* Connects to Duncan Jones' *Moon*', *Den of Geek* (February 2018)

Lacan, Jacques, 'The Mirror Stage as formative of the function of the I as revealed in psychoanalytic experience', *Écrits: A Selection* (1949)

Little, Henry; 'For All Mankind: A Brief Cultural History of the Moon', *The White Review* (September 2013)

MacKinnon, Angus, 'The Future Isn't What It Used to Be', *NME* (13 September 1980)

McCarthy, Erin, 'Questions for Duncan Jones, Director of the Film *Moon*', *Popular Mechanics* (October 2009)

'*Moon* is Duncan Jones' Homage to Classic Sci-Fi', *Wired* (July 2009)

Owen, Jeremy, 'Gavin Rothery talks *Moon* (2009)', filminutiae.com (no date)

Rothery, Gavin, 'Designing Sarang: Robotic Space-House of the Future', gavinrothery.com (21 August 2011)

Springer, Katherine, 'Hard Science Fiction in Film: Analyzing Duncan Jones's *Moon*', *Film Matters* (Winter 2012)

Stoate, Robin, '"We're not programmed, we're people": Figuring the caring computer', *Feminist Theory*, 13.2 (August 2012)

Stoker, Jez, 'Archive: Interview with Film Writer/Director Gavin Rothery', BorrowingTape.com (no date)

Sundvall, Scott, 'Clonetrolling the Future: Body, Space, and Ontology in Duncan Jones' *Moon* and Mark Romanek's *Never Let Me Go*', *Politics of Place*, 2 (16 March 2015)

Wiegel, Alexander, 'AI in Science-Fiction: A Comparison of *Moon* (2009) and *2001: A Space Odyssey* (1968)', *Aventius Visio*, 28.4 (2012)

MEDIA

Fowler, Jeremy and Phelim O'Neill, 'Making of *Moon*', Electronic Press Kit, *Moon* DVD (2010)

Jones, Duncan; 'Science Center Q&A with Director Duncan Jones', *Moon* DVD (2010)

Gavin Rothery website: gavinrothery.com

www.ingramcontent.com/pod-product-compliance
Lightning Source LLC
Chambersburg PA
CBHW071413300426
44114CB00016B/2287